"Marriage,
Seeing it
God's Way"

"Marriage,
Seeing it
God's Way"

Dedicated to my Wife
Minister Cassandra Y. Cooper

ELDER VICTOR R. COOPER

authorHOUSE®

AuthorHouse™ LLC
1663 Liberty Drive
Bloomington, IN 47403
www.authorhouse.com
Phone: 1-800-839-8640

Published by AuthorHouse   08/30/2013

ISBN: 978-1-4918-0164-2 (sc)
ISBN: 978-1-4918-0166-6 (hc)
ISBN: 978-1-4918-0165-9 (e)

Library of Congress Control Number: 2013913534

Contents

Contents

Special Acknowledgement

First, I give honor to my Lord and Savior Jesus Christ for giving me the wisdom and knowledge to pen this book. I realize we can do nothing in our own strength, "We can do all things through Christ which strengthens us." We only get one chance at life, who we meet in life can have a life changing impact on our lives for ever. Therefore, I like to give special thanks to a few people who made a different in my life with their love and friendship.

I truly thank God for my former pastor and founder of Praise Temple Apostolic Faith Church of Virginia, D/E Vernon L. Spinks and Co-Pastor Phillystine C. Spinks, of Praise Temple of Raleigh, N.C., Elder Samuel Cooper and Jacqueline Cooper, founder of Highest Praise Church Greensboro, N.C., Elder Terrence S. Brown for his moral support. I like to mention a few special friends who inspired me and encouraged me to move forward with this project. Min. Charles Murrell Jr., Sis. Mary L. Armentrout, and Bro. Gerald Boyd. I thank God for their support, fellowship and stellar friendship. The Bible says, "A man that hath friends must shew himself friendly: and there is a friend that sticketh closer than a brother."

Also, to the anointed men of God who the Lord charged to sow into me the Word of God, the Bible says, "Give honor to whom honor is due." I appreciated their labor of love, patient and tutelage of the infallible words of the Lord. My apostolic father

D/E Frank Worsham pastor of Church of Christ Apostolic, Amelia, Va., Bishop Raymond Faison Jr. pastor of Church of God and True Holiness, Fredericksburg, Va., Bishop Dr. John T. Leslie Jr. author of "Everybody Can't Be Right" pastor of Church of Jesus Christ, Washington, D.C., he is the Dioceses of the ESSC of the P.C.A.F. Bishop Dr. Jarrett Mickie author of "Broken" pastor and founder of New Light Cathedral, Thornburg, Va., Bishop Dr. Gilbert H. Edwards author of "The Tabernacle & The Priesthood and there Functions" pastor of The Full Gospel True Mission, Baltimore, Md., and Elder Dr. Daniel Ahia-Armah author of six books "Riding the Winds of Change", "Victory Technique", "Goliath can Fall", Seven Effects of Prayer", "The Stone Seal & Soldiers". I like to give special thanks to my family and my wife family for all their support throughout the years, especially Ms. Sylvia Dunston a God sent sister-in-law who showed us great hospitality to stay over night at her home for many, many years. Thank you all.

Dedication

For my lovely wife who I believe is a special gift from
God, she was made especially for me. God have blessed us to
be together for thirty years and every day is better than the day
before. Cassandra, you are a special jewel to me, thank you for
allowing God to use you in keeping the flames going in our lives.
Many times when I was wrong in the past you never said once,
"I told you so". I am so graceful you allowed the Holy Ghost to
work things out between us without arguing or fighting. Honey, I
appreciate your love, patient, support and anointed prayers during
the time I was researching and writing this manuscript. I know it
was a sacrifice for you personally, one year prior I was working on
my master degree. I could never repay you for that, that's a debt I
will forever owe you, your love and gratitude is worth more than
money can ever buy. I will never forget the nights when I was sick
you prayed for my healing, I thank God for a save and praying
wife the next day or so I felt much better. "The effectual fervent
prayer of the righteous man availeth much" (James 5:16).

Thank you for putting up with me for countless numbers of
hours on the computer late nights, when we could have spent
some quite time together. I can say with a degree of certainty,
you consistently reminded me of my husband duties, it caused
me to work faster to complete this project. I remember your favor
line which keeps ringing in my ears "God did not tell the wife to
love her husband, but the husband to love his wife." Because you
continue to say those words to me it caused me to add a chapter to

the book "Husband lead your Wife's", you open new prospective and avenue how a husband should respect, love and cleave to his wife. Without you this chapter would not have been written for this book. "All things do work together for the good."

To my father the late Nathaniel (Dad) Cooper Sr., thank you for being there when I needed you the most. Dad, you taught me so many things, but one thing stood out the most, how to be a responsible man. The moments we shared together and the lessons of life you taught me concerning manhood I will forever pondered them in my heart. No woman could have taught me that, no woman will ever be able to teach a boy how to be a man. You said to me, "A man is not a man by age alone, but real men take responsibility as head of their house and provide for his family even when you must deny your self personal things for the good of the family. I believe in my heart if you were not in the home I think I would have become a statistic (high school dropout, on drug, or a drug dealer) like many other young black males. All those verbal warning along with the beating brought discipline into my life and it made me the person who I am today. "Now no chastening for the present seemeth to be joyous, but grievous: nevertheless afterward it yieldeth the peaceable fruit of righteousness unto them which are exercised thereby" (Heb. 12:11). Dad thanks for been that positive role model, great mentor, but most of all, my best friend. I'll never forget these words you said to me, "love your family, pray every day, work hard and respect others." I will for ever love you, thanks.

Introduction

Many friends have asked me the same question over and over again, why write a book of marriage when there's so many out there on this subject? My answer is simply this, I was inspired by God to share with the people of God and the secular world God's expectation on a covenant marriage "one man and one woman for life".

The truth on marriage according to the way God see it. The book "Marriage, seeing it God's Way" will reward you in many ways spiritually and naturally. We serve a God who is holy, righteous and change not; nothing God do is ever in question because it is perfect.

Sovereign, the scope of His rule is transcendent, that is, not only does it includes the entire physical universe, but it exceeds it. He existed before all creation, he expands beyond it, He compasses all that it is. The power by which He rules is exercised by his will, His works and His word. For example, by His works his spirit displays his unlimited power and, by His own words he spoke creation into existence. His authority to rule is in his preexistence and Holiness.

Thus, as it creator, He deserves to be its Potentate (King). His benevolent intent in creating things "good" reveal His holy nature (that is, complete and perfect), and this His moral right to be creation's King.

I find it amazing so many people in the Christian society believes in marriage, but also in divorce. "Out of the same mouth proceedeth blessing and cursing. My brethren these things ought not so to be" (James 3:10).

It is truly an honor to say, the Bible have a crystal definition of marriage and divorce. Throughout this book it will reveal God's truth for man and woman in an inseparable bond in the unity of marriage. Why polygamy, adultery and divorce is a distortion of the marriage covenant, it have permeated itself through history, cultures and society. But, as the Lord Jesus said, ". . . from the beginning it was not so" (Matt. 19:8). Marriage is not an invention of man. God instituted and orchestrated marriage with divine implication. Divorce and polygamy was never sanction by or approved of God. Jesus said, "Moses because of the hardness of your hearts suffered [permitted] you to put away your wives . . ." (Matt. 19:8).

Marriage is an institution of God and is a continuation of His work of creation. Sexual desires are God-given. We should view our manliness or womanliness as a gift from God which we ought to receive with thankfulness and strive to keep holy and pure in accordance with His instruction. First, man and woman are to remain virgin until marriage. After marriage one is to have sexual relations only with their marriage partner period. Sexual relations outside of marriage is adultery, which was also punishable by death under the Old Covenant (laws of Moses). To preserve the sanctity of marriage and the well being of man, God has established certain laws regarding sexual activities. God wants marriage to be preserved for husband and wife only. Any other sexual activities prior to marriage are also forbidden by God and are referred to as fornication, a sin which carries the death penalty under the Old Covenant law. "Let not sin therefore reign in your mortal body, that ye should obey it in the lusts thereof" (Romans 6:12).

This is a true fact, with marriage as well as with all other human activities, "God hath made man upright; but they have sought out many inventions [schemes]" (Ecclesiastes 7:29). The point is this; men are more virtuous than women. But that, while God created humanity upright, both men and women have defiled themselves. As a result, there are none without blame. From this come polygamy, adultery, easy divorce and same sex marriages. Hosea said, "My people are destroyed for the lack of knowledge: because thou hast rejected knowledge, I will also reject thee, that thou shalt be no priest to me: seeing thou hast forgotten the law of they God, I will also forget thy children" (Hosea 4:6).

When a man and woman comes together in marriage it is because they believe they can better serve God together as husband and wife, not to satisfy themselves sexually, nor for the purpose of leaving the home life or for finance security. I pray this book will bless you, enlighten you and transform your life seeing marriage as God designed it to be. Every young lady is not called to be a wife and every young man is not meant to be a husband. Apostle said, "For I would that all men were even as I myself. But every man hath his proper gift of God, one after this manner, and another after that. I say therefore to the unmarried and widows. It is good for them if they abide even as I" (1 Corinthians 7:7-8).

Marriage is a commitment for life if you are not ready to submit yourself, deny yourself, or give up your personal agenda for your spouse, my advice to you is do not rush into it. Seek the Lord diligently and wait on Him 'he shall direct your path'. Do not allow the enemy (Devil) to cause you to fall into his snare convincing you it time to marry, once you make that decision it's a vow unto death. Jesus said, "adultery and whoremonger he will judge".

Apostle Peter said,

> "For it had been better for them not have known the way of righteousness, than, after they have known it, to turn from the holy command-ment delivered unto them" (2 Peter 2:21).

Marriage is a holy union in the presence of God where two people man and woman coming together to commit themselves contractual to each other in the sight of witnesses for the purpose of been husband and wife. This divine union is for life, because it is divine the devil try to throw so many obstacles in your way to try and derail the marriage. I want to let you; "it's only a test" no weapon formed against you shall prosper. At all cost stay together, cleave to one another "one can chase a thousand, two can put ten thousand to flight" (Deut. 32:30). "Where there is unity, there is strength." Remember, the devil goal is to destroy all marriages, through confusion, disruption and using past history to create division, separation and finally divorce. "Jesus said, "What therefore God hath joined together, let not man put asunder" (Matt. 19:6).

As you read through this book bear in mind marriage is of God, no matter whether you saved or unsaved as long as they are equally yoke together. The Bible says, "Marriage is honourable in all, and the bed undefiled" (Hebrews 13:4). I believe the word "All" means all who marry, God have no respecter person. This is a moral law of God's, which includes all who take the wedding vows. According to God's law which is the Word of God man's law should not supersede what God have established without penalty of judgment. In Matthew Jesus makes a very strong statement in regards to his word, "Heaven and earth shall pass away, but my words shall not pass away." It is clearly written in John 17:17 when Jesus said, "Thy word is truth." Psalm 119:89 states, "For ever, O Lord, thy word is settled in heaven".

Five important points you should consider before co-habitation with a man or woman:

(1) Living together your relationship with your significant other changes the moment you marry. You have now made a commitment to each other as husband and wife in front of almost everyone significant in your life.

(2) Words matter. They deeply affect us and others. Living with your "boy-friend" is not the same as living with your "husband." And living with your "girlfriend" or any other title you give her is not the same as making a home with your "wife."

(3) Legality matters. Being legally bond to and responsible for another person matters. It is an announcement to him/her and to yourself that you take this relationship with the utmost seriousness.

(4) To better appreciate just how important marriage is to the vast majority of people in your life, consider this: There is no event, no occasion, no mo-ment in your life when so many of the people who matter to you will con-vene in one place as they will at your wedding.

(5) Only with marriage will your man's or your woman's family ever be-comes your family. The two weddings transformed the woman in my son's life into my daughter-in-law and transformed the man in my daughter's life into my son-in-law. And I was instantly transformed from the father of their boyfriend or girlfriend into their father-in-law.

I find it pretty profound to see an educated society disputing over the same following issues for centuries. (a) Marriage, (b) who can marriage and (3 if divorce permitted by God. The Creator words are like an arrow straight and go forward. Genesis 2:24 says, "Therefore, shall a man [singular and a male] leave his father and his mother, and shall cleave unto his wife [singular and a female]; and they shall be one flesh. You find in the pages of this book marriage is between one man and one woman, divorce and polygamy is not permitted by God, finally homosexuality is abomination in the sight of God.

Chapter 1

Marriage According to God

How do we define <u>Marriage?</u> Merriam Webster defines it this way—"the formal union of a man and a woman typically recognized by law, by which they become husband and wife. A relationship between married people or the period for which it will last." (The state of being united to a person of the opposite sex as husband and wife in a consensual and contractual relationship recognized by state laws).

Notice the negative connotation in the definition "the period for which it will lasts" Is there a spoken prophecy in the definition? Think on that.

According to scriptures, <u>Marriage</u> is a describe covenant contract between God and man, the joining together one man to one woman before witnesses in the presence of God exchanging vows. "Wherefore they are no more twain, but one flesh. What therefore God hath joined together, let not man put asunder" (Matt. 19:6).

The Lord God preformed the first marriage Adam and Eve in the Garden of Eden. Man and woman marital unity were in God's infinite plan from the foundation of the world. In Genesis 1: 26 "And God said, Let us make man in our image, after our likeness: and let them have dominion . . . ." As it is written God made man on the six day. "So God created man in his own image, in the image of God created he him; male and female created he them. And God blessed them, and God said unto them, Be fruitful, and multiply, and replenish [fill] the earth, and subdue it" (Genesis 1:28-29).

After Adam had named all the animals there were no help meet for him, God in his compassion for Adam, said, "it not good that man should be alone; I will make him a help meet for him [helper comparable to him]." And the Lord God caused a deep sleep to fall upon Adam. And he slept: and he took one of his ribs, and closed up the flesh instead thereof. And the rib which the Lord God had taken from man, made he a woman [singular], and brought her unto the man" (Genesis 2:21-22). This divine intervention represents the joining together man and woman as husband and wife. Adam later confirmed it with the following words; "This is now bone of my bones, and flesh of my flesh: she shall be called woman, because she was taken out of Man" (Genesis 2:23). The joining together of Adam in Eve is an eternal and Holy marriage for life. "Therefore shall a man leave his father and his mother, and shall cleave [be joined] unto his wife: and they shall be one flesh" (Genesis 2:24). No man can separate his flesh from body and yet live, marriage is meant to be a life long union together as husband and wife until death.

I like what Jay E. Adams said in his book "Marriage, Divorce and Remarriage." Contrary to much contemporary thought and teaching, marriage is not a human expedience. It was not devised by man; but it was corrupted by men in the per-meated of history, cultures and society. God in his excellent and unlimited power created the martial institution between man and woman. If marriage were a human origin, then human beings should have a right to set the standards and determine who and how it should be establish. However, since God designed this covenant relationship between man and woman He is the author, therefore God's rules and his precepts applies to all of humanity (believers and unbelievers) alike.

Dr. Norman Geisler, is an evangelical Christian scholar who is author and co-author of over fifty Christian books writes, "marriage involves a covenant before God between one man and one woman." Marriage does not only involves a physical attraction between male and female but includes a conjugal (sexual) rights, it is a union born of a covenant of mutual promises. Both party promise to love, care and support each other until death due them part. They have taken vows before wit-nesses and in the presence of the God, "God honor your vows."

The Book of Ecclesiastes 5:5 states,

> "Better is it that thous shouldest not vow, than that
> thou shouldest vow and not pay."

> If a man vow a vow unto the Lord, or swear an
> oath to bind his soul with with a bond; he shall
> not break his word, he shall do according to all
> that proceedeth out of his mouth. If a woman also
> vow a vow unto the Lord, and bind herself by a
> bond, being in her father's house in her youth; and
> her father hear her vow, and her bond wherewith
> she hath bound her soul, and her father shall hold

his peace at her: than all he vows shall stand, and
every bond wherewith she hath bound her soul shall
stand" (Numb. 30:2-4).

The Book of Malachi 2:14 states,

". . . Because the Lord has been a witness between
thee and the wife of thy youth, against whom thou
hast dealt treacherously: yet is she thy com-panion,
and the wife of thy covenant."

According to this passage of Scripture it is evidence that
companion describes a permanent partnership by the covenant, the
union of a marriage is formal, public, legal, and sacred, a binding
contract. Geisler goes on to say, marriage is a God ordained
institution for all people not just for Christians only. Marriage
is the only social institution God planned before creation of
humanity for the purpose of pro-creation.

Holman wrote in his commentary dictionary, "Because God
instituted marriage, marriage is more than just a ceremony; but it is
based on a life long covenant or oath sworn before God".

"Nevertheless I will remember my covenant with
thee in the days of thy youth, and I will establish
unto thee an everlasting covenant" (Ezekiel 16:60)

Neither private individuals nor the states have the authority
to dissolve what God have ordained. Many states have made

legislations to determine what marriage is, who can marry, and when should marriage end in divorce.

No matter what man's legislate into law, how society accepts one's life style, or what individuals may think, God said marriage is between one man and one woman. When God made man he also made him a help meet she looked like Adam but she was different yet a perfect match for Adam. In marriage, a man is to leave his family, join his wife, and unite with her. The word joined speaks of both a physical embrace and more general aspects of marital bonding. In marriage, man and wo-man is a "we," not just a "me and you". One flesh suggests both a physical, sexual bonding and a lifelong relationship. There are still two persons, but together they are as one (husband and wife). What man lacked she [woman] supplied, and what she lacked he [man] supplied. The culmination was one flesh the complete unity of man and woman in marriage. God is perfect He makes no mistakes, when He put Adam and Eve together it was an implication that marriage involves one male and one female becoming "one flesh" for life.

God sets the standard how man should conduct themselves according to His Moral Laws. Moral law is a system of guidelines for behavior underpinning the morality of a civilization. "Moses' Ten Commandments are moral laws to govern humanity. Many of our ethical principles held primarily by Christian throughout history have influenced the development of U.S. secular laws. Actually, the U.S. constitution is written off biblical principles. No men law exceeds the Laws of God.

"Thou shalt not lie with mankind, as with womankind: it is abomination"

(Leviticus 18:23).

"And if a man also lie with mankind, as he lieth with a woman, both of them have committed an abomination: they shall surely be put to death; their blood shall be upon them" (Leviticus 20:13).

Apostle Paul said,

"Likewise also the men, leaving the natural **use** of the woman, burned in their lust for one another, men with men committing what is shameful, and receiving in themselves the penalty of their error which was due (Romans 1:27 KJV Study Bible).

"Who, knowing the righteous judgment of God, that those who practice such things are deserving of death, not only do the same but also approve of those who practice them (Romans 1:32 KJV Study Bible).

There's a penalty "judgment" for going outside of the will and laws of God, man and woman is meant to be together in the bond and unity of marriage. Any other marriage except between man and woman is not accepted by God, regardless if man voted it into state or local law. It falls out of the realm of God's purpose for man and woman in procreation.

Chapter 2

Who can Marry who?

This may seen to be a rhetoric question but society as a whole is transforming what was once sound ethical principles of marriage between man and woman into a society free fall without moral values (chaos). It is the consensual of many church groups marriage is both a natural institution and a sacred union. It is rooted in God's plan from creation. The truth is, marriage can only exist between a man and a woman woven deeply into the human spirit. The Church's teaching on marriage expresses a truth, therefore, that can be perceived first and foremost by human reason. This truth has been confirmed by divine Revelation in Sacred Scripture, according to the article in www.foryourmarriage.org.

The institution of marriage has gone through major social ideas and developments. Many of these are related to our contemporary understanding about the equality of men and women. These conflicting developments have created division in the mind of average citizens. The question is has it enhanced or devalue the basic purpose and nature of marriage. To accept or legalize same sex marriage would radically redefine marriage according to the Word of God. This question needs to be answer by the massive of society and not simply as individuals. I believe with a degree of certainty, if same sex marriage were legalized, the result would be a significant change in our social value. I further believe it would send a false message, saying, the primary purpose of marriage is to validate and protect a sexuality intimate relationship. All else would be less important. Even though, we can not say exactly what effects it will have I seriously believe it will be negatively. For one, marriage will no longer symbolize a godly institution or holy union between man and woman. Therefore, it would symbolize a commitment to the present needs and desires of ones lust of the flesh, which is ungodly according to the article "Between Man and Woman".

The general argument is this; the church is discriminating against homosexual people by opposing same sex union. No, in defense of church Christian must stand firm on the principles of the written Word of God, the church is required to uphold the precepts of God statutes against immoral behavior and practices. Because of immoral behavior in Sodom and Gomorrah God destroyed those cities.

> "And they called unto Lot, and said unto him, where are the men which came in to thee this nigh? Bring them out unto us, that we may <u>know</u> [carnally] them" (Genesis 19:5).

According to the commentary in the New King James Version he says, "The word <u>know</u> is to be interpreted as carnal or sexual knowledge, here referring to homo-sexuality. The scripture clearly denounces homosexuality as sin. Under the law Leviticus 18:22-30 declare homosexuality a capital offense, punishable by death (stoning to death).

Apostle Paul said,

> Know ye not that the unrighteous shall not inherit
> the kingdom of God? Be not deceived, neither
> fornicators [the sexually immoral], nor idolaters,
> nor adulterers, nor effeminate [homosexuals],
> nor abusers of themselves with man-kind . . ." (1
> Corinthians 6:9).

To interpret the above Scripture, it simply means—"do not lie with a man as one lies with a woman, that is detestable [abomination], the woman is not to lie with woman as one lies with a man."

It is not unjust to deny legal status to same-sex unions because God do not honor that type of marriage, same-sex unions are contrary to God Holiness.

The legal recognition of marriage includes benefits. To be associated with the benefits it doesn't require a personal commitment, but the social commitment a husband and wife makes is contribute to the well-being of society. To redefine marriage for the sake of providing benefits to those who cannot rightfully enter into marriage would be wrong too. As a matter of fact, some benefits currently sought after by individual in homosexual unions can already be obtained without regard to marital status. "i.e. individual can agree to own property jointly, and they can chose any one they desire to be beneficiary of their will or to make health care decision in case they become income-potent."

Allow me to attempt to explain why same-sex union is not equivalent to a marriage ordained by God. (1) Same-sex union contradicts the nature and purpose of marriage, procreation, only a man and a woman can reproduce a godly seed, (2) They can not enter into a true conjugal union, it is wrong to equate their relationship to a marriage, it cannot achieve the natural purpose of sexual union. God never intended for man and man or woman and woman to marry it is not His divine will, God do all things "decently and in order." As a matter of fact, God called it immoral and abomination in his sight.

The Bible says,

> "Whoso findeth a wife findeth a good thing, and
> obtaineth favour of the Lord (Proverbs 18:22).

The relationship of Christ to His church is illustrated by that of a husband to his wife. Christ is called the Bridegroom and His church is called the bride. Christ loved the church and gave Himself for it, that He might sanctify, cleanse, and glorify it.

This is another divine order of God reference to husband and wife in the Book of Ephesians 5:22-25,

> "Wives, submit yourselves unto your own husbands,
> as unto the Lord. For the husband is the head of the
> wife, even as Christ is the head of the church: and
> he is the savior of the body. Therefore as the church
> is subject unto Christ, so let the wives be to their

own husbands in every thing. Husbands, love your
wives, even as Christ also loved the church, and
gave himself for it."

Apostle Paul said,

"Neither was the man created for the woman; but
the woman for the man" (1 Corinthians 11:9).

Chapter 3

When should you get Marry?

Apostle Paul said, "If they cannot contain [exercise self control], let them marry: for it is better to marry than to burn [burn with passion]." Paul said, "I say this as a concession, not as a command. I wish that all men were as I am. But each man his own gift from; one has this gift, another has that" (1 Corinthians 7:6-7 NIV Study Bible).

Exactly what age is the right age to get married? The Bible do not speak of an age limit, this question has been debated by many and resolved by none. In today's society young people are waiting later to get married. Marriage is life changing. When you get married your life will change a great deal. Do not take it lightly, there are many areas of marriage that requires sacrifice, denying yourself is top priority, you learn to work together for the good of the family and not self. It changes your entire life and ways you can never image, if you are not ready to sacrifice your own agenda you are not ready for marriage. As a matter of fact, 60% of all couple who marry between the ages of 20 and 25 divorces, according the article in the National Healthy Marriage Resource Center in Oklahoma City, Ok. (Info@HealtyMariageInfo.org). Before entering into a marital covenant you should do a self evaluation asking yourself these questions. (1) I'm I taking marriage serious as God meant it to be. (2) Is God the center focus, or flesh? And, (3) Do you know enough about him/her, personal history, finances, health, work, spiritual belief, family and credit history.

One thing for sure, maturity spiritual makes for a happier marriages and a stable relationship. Most couples who understand God principles of the marital union live their lives in fear of God and submit their selves to one another forsaking self most likely lead to a healthy and lasting marriage. We must have enough maturity to look beyond the here and now and be able to commit ourselves to joining with this one person for the rest of your life in the fear of God. You have to understand marriage requires sacrifice and unselfishness. Before marrying couple should plan and determining what roles and duties their going assume in the marriage. It is necessary to check out the history of your mate prior to coming together as husband and wife. These are few things you may need to know about your mate.

1. Do you believe in prayer, fasting, studying the Word of God, attending church.
2. Know what spiritual goals, values and moral principles he/she have.
3. God focus and not worldly focus.
4. Educational back ground, career goals, if employed with whom.
5. Financially sound credit worthy.
6. Living arrangement.
7. Any bad habits (drug, gambling and spending).
8. Ability to share.
9. Know your mate family health, mental & criminal history.
10. Make sure there is no kids

"Let no man deceive himself if any among you
seemeth to be wise in this world, let him become
a fool, that he many be wise. For the wisdom of
this world is foolishness with God" (1Corinthians
3:18-19).

When should one get married? There is no right time to get
marry. Marriage is different for each person and unique in every
situation. There is a level of maturity one must develop before
venturing into a life bidding commitment. Even though we grow
and mature at different stages of life some far later than others it do
not change God's expectation of the union between husband and
wife.

Life experiences are varying factors, some people are ready
for marriage at age 18, and others are never ready for it. A strong
foundation is imperative for a successful marriage and should be
settled before one even begins to date or court a potential life mate.

A person must know what the Bible says about love,
commitment, sexual relations, the role of a husband and wife, and
God expectations of us before committing to marriage. Have at
least one Christian married couple as a mentor or role model is
valuable, it gives one the opportunity to learn from and imitate.
Older couple can answer many questions because of experience
and direct you what course of action to take regarding marital
issues. One of the key ingredients in problem solving is know your
partner well and understand their moods and the way respond to
crisis's. You should know each other views on marriage, finances,

in-laws, child-rearing, discipline, duties of a husband and wife. Try to Know each other level of spiritual maturity and commitment to the Word of God, do take an individual word examine them for yourself over a period of time. If you find out later, it maybe too late. "Know them which labour among you" (1Thessalonians 5:12).

One author said, marriage is divine and honorable in the presence of God, before one decide to get marry it must be a clear conscience that both can better serve God as a couple than an individual. You should never enter into a marriage with the idea divorce is an option, not even as the last straw. Marriage is not only a commitment, but a covenant with God. A promise was vow to remain with that person for the rest of your life, no matter what. A Christian marriage should endure through every circumstance, angering, hardship, disaster, depression, bitterness, addiction, and loneliness. The Bible tells us that through God all things are possible (Luke 18:27), and this certainly includes staying married.

One interesting point I like to make, do not get consumed with the idea of a "perfect mate" there is none, the Bible does not speak of it, nor give an example of one. The one thing God's Word does explicitly tell us, not be "unequally yoke together with an unbeliever" (2 Corinthians 6:14). Even though we are free to marry whoever we please Apostle Paul makes it crystal in chapter 7 and verse 39 in 1 Corinthians "The wife is bound by the law as long as her husband liveth; but if her husband be dead, she is at liberty to be married to whom she will; only in the Lord." It is not fruitful for a believer to be bounded together in a relationship with a nonbeliever this could weaken ones Christian commitment, integrity and standard of holiness.

God told King Solomon and Israel in 1 King 11:2-4 not to marry strange wives for they will turn your hearts to their gods. "For it came to pass, when Solomon was old, that his wives turned away his heart after other gods; and his heart was not perfect with the Lord his God, as was the heart of David his father" (1 King 11:4). Therefore it is crucial to be in a relationship with someone with like faith, who attends a church consistently, active in the ministry, enjoys fellowshipping with the saints of God (Acts 2:42), and study the Bible faithfully daily.

After completion of premarital counseling (sessions) with your pastor it should be determined at that point in the relationship if want to continue with the wedding arrangements. If you both believe it's going to work out move forward with the wedding plans. If you had a pastor who was willing to marry you without marital counseling find another pastor immediately there is some thing wrong with him spiritually. During your marital sessions many things should have been exposed and talk about to decide if the relationship need to continue moving forward or be delayed. A wedding should not go forward is there is some issues with credit, criminal record, and past history with a pervious relationship involving children. If all things sound, ask the pastor to pray for God's blessing and continue with the wedding plans. God will make all things ready in it time. Therefore, "earnestly seek the will of God, He will direct our path" (Proverbs 3:5-6). After you have weighed all options and allowed the Holy Spirit to cultivate both through the Word of God go in faith. Remember, marriage is an every lasting love commitment. Not the "Philia love" which is a brotherly emotionally type of love man sent; but in the "Agapa love" which is from God.

When you have agape love for your partner your time for marriage is closer now than ever before. "Love is patient, love is kind. It does not envy, it does not boast, it is not proud. It is not rude, it is not self-seeking, it is not easily angered, and it keeps no record of wrongs. Love does not delight in evil but rejoices with the truth. It always protects, always trusts, always hopes, and always perseveres." When you find yourself ready to love another person like that, it is the right time for marriage. I can say with a degree of certainty, the Lord will confirm your marriage through your spiritual leader. When that time comes all things will be made ready and set in order for the wedding to take place, no stones in the matter will be left unturned all things will work together for the good. Seek the Lord while He can be found, and ask Him for his divine guidance and then wait upon the Lord. God is the author of all things He knows when the best time and right time for you to marry. He is the past, the future and the presence wait on Him. One last fruit though, when God do something it lasts, "What you do for Christ last." God will not allow you to be in a disruptive or a bad situation unless you are out of His will, stepping out on your own will. Psalm 1:1 says, "Blessed is the man that walketh not in the counsel of the ungodly, nor standeth in the way of sinners, nor sitteth in the seat of the scornful."

Chapter 4

Is Polygamy Permitted by God?

What is polygamy? A marriage involving multiplies spouses instead of only one. Polygamy has been practiced for many centuries; it has been eliminated in most modern countries and from their societies. While polygamy is illegal in the United States, it is still practiced in many others areas around the world. In fact, bigamy is sometime used interchangeably with polygamy. Although they are not necessarily the same thing they are similar. Bigamy technically means having 2 spouses at the same time, but they are separately married and each spouse does not know the other. The concept of polygamy tends to be a fertile issue for controversial debate. Some claim polygamy is a religious tenet; other sees it as a matter of choice with no religious implication at all. They believe it is unhealthy living which could lead to an unbalanced society. Looking at it from a rearview mirror it may lead to men not wanting a potential mate, which it could devalue the family structure of God's work husband, wife and procreation?

Contrary to widespread opinion, the Bible does not speak strongly against polygamy neither in the Old Testament or the New Testament. There is mountains of evident from many passages of Scriptures God is against it. For instant, Genesis 2:18 "And the Lord God said, It is not good that the man should be alone; I will make him a help [helper comparable to him] meet for him." The word 'help' in the Scripture mean one (singular). Genesis 2:22 states "And the rib [singular], which the Lord God had taken from man, made he a woman [singular], and brought her unto the man."

To be joined together as husband and wife. "And Adam said, "This is now bone of my bones [she belong to him], and flesh of my flesh; she shall be called woman [given her his name], because she was taken out of man" (Genesis 2:23). Adam was the first man and Eve was the first woman and the entire human race came from them in the beginning. God's ideal plan for marriage is one man for one woman for one lifetime. "Therefore shall a man leave his father and his mother, and shall cleave unto his wife [singular]: and they shall be one flesh" (Genesis 2:24). The pattern God have for marital happiness is evident when a man loves and leads his family, the wife reverence him and the children obey him (Ephesians 5:21-23; 6:1). God gave Adam only one wife this set the precedent for the whole human race to imitate. "You shall not covet your neighbor's wife" (Exodus 20:17). God made it a commandment for man not to seek after his neighbor's wife, it was unlaw-ful to do so. Some people refer to the Scripture in the Book of Kings to support their point God allowed polygamy with King Solomon.

The writer of www.gotquestions.org Willard F. Harley states, even while God allowed polygamy because of the hardness of their hearts God's judgment was activated against those who practiced it. "And the Lord was angry with Solomon, because his heart was turned from the Lord God of Israel, which had appeared unto him twice" (1 Kings 11:9). "Wherefore the Lord said unto Solomon, Forasmuch as this is done of thee, and thou hast not kept my covenant and my statutes, which I have commanded thee, I will surely rend [tear away] the kingdom from thee, and will give it to thy servant" (1 Kings 11:12). Not only that, God stirred up adversaries against Solomon kingdom. "And the Lord stirred up an adversary unto Solomon, Hadad the Edomite: he was of the king's seed in Edom" (1 Kings 11:14).

I find it interesting no one never refer to the Scripture in Deuteronomy 17:17 which states, "Neither shall he multiply wives to himself, that his heart turn not away."

The first practice of polygamy occurred in the descendants of Cain, one who was under the curse of Yahweh (Lord of Host) for the murder of his brother Abel. You would expect ones out of God's will not to follow the percepts of God because of the curse nature attached to their lives. "When men began to multiply on the face of the earth, and daughters were born unto them [Cain descendants], that the sons of God [Seth descendants] saw the daughters of men that they were fair; and they took them wives of all which they chose" (Genesis 6:1-2). When the sons of God came in unto the daughters of men, and they bare children to them, the same became mighty men which were of old, men of renown. And God [the Lord] saw that the wicked-ness of man was great in the earth, and that every imagination of the thoughts of his heart was only evil continually. It repented the Lord that he had made man on the earth, and it grieved him at his heart. And the Lord said, I will destroy man whom I have created from the face of the earth" (Genesis 6:4-7). All sin is punishable by God, having more than one wife is wicked in God's sight. Polygamy [more specifically "polygamy"] was related to an abnormal development of the family as viewed by God. Lamech of the Old Testament was the first polygamy also was of the seed [descendant] of Cain [who was cursed] probably was the force behind the world been destroyed the first time. Polygamy never casts a positive shadow in the Scriptures, but a source of negative bitter rivalry and bickering within families. Apostle Paul makes in clear in the New Testament Scriptures one man and one woman in marriage when he wrote to the church in Corinth. Apostle Paul was asked several questions on the subject of marriage by the church.

Apostle Paul said,

> "Now concerning the things whereof ye wrote unto me: It is good for a man not to touch a woman. Nevertheless, to avoid fornication, let every man have his own wife [singular], and let every woman have her own husband [singular]" (1 Corinthians 7:1-2).

I like the way Jesus refer to the church [singular] as His bride.

> "Wives, submit yourselves unto your own husbands, as unto the Lord. For the husband is the head of the wife [singular], even as Christ is the head of the church: and he is the savior of the body. Therefore as the church is sub-ject unto Christ, so let the wives be to their own husbands in every thing" (Ephesians 5:22-24).

During the early stages of man the law of God was not always respected or followed, but all sin will be judged by God. In the Book of Malachi chapter 2 and verses 14-15 states,

"Yet ye say, Wherefore? Because the Lord hath
been witness between thee and the wife of thy
youth, against who thou hast dealt treacherously:
yet is she thy companion, and the wife of thy
covenant. And did not he make one? Yet had he
the residue of the spirit. And wherefore one? That
he might seek a godly seed. Therefore take heed to
your spirit, and let none deal treacherously against
the wife of his youth.

When God choose the Israelites (the Jews) as His chosen
people from the days of Abraham to be in covenant relationship
with Him, he never made any other nations His people. One bride
for one groom, Jesus is the ultimate example the church only is
the Bride of Christ, we are to follow Him. After the sacrificial
system for forgiving sins was in place, Moses instructed the
people on God's standard of Holy Living. Marrying relatives was
prohibited by God for physical, social and moral reasons. Children
born to near relatives may experience serious health problems.
Without these specific laws, sexual promiscuity would have been
more likely, first in families, then outside. When improper sexual
relations begin family life is destroyed (Leviticus 18:9-18). For
example; when Abram wife Sarai could not bare him a children
she gave her handmaid to Abram to go in unto her maid Hagar.
And when she (Hagar) saw that she had conceived, her mistress
was despised in her eyes [sight]. Sarai spoke to Abram and said the
following, "I have given my maid into thy bosom, and when she
saw that she had conceived I was despised in her eyes" (Genesis
16:5).

Genesis 16:6 "But Abram said unto Sarai, behold,
thy maid is in thy hand do to her as it pleaseth thee.
And when Sarai dealt hardly with her, she fled from
her face".

Then Hagar and her son Ishmael were put out of Abram home
to journey to another land. There can only be one king in his
castle, the king can have only one queen, if there is any other it
will creates confusion and disruption. There will be no peace in
the home, because fleshly pride will stir up jealous, jealous envy,
and envy strife which means chaos. That is not an environment to
rear up children and then expect them to grow up with a positive
and healthy mental attitude. Is it possible? Yes, more than likely
some form of psychological effect will occur in their life which can
impact his/her decision and though process mentally.

One final notice, polygamy introduces incest in family which
causes emotional and mental problems, by combining the same
biological genes (DNA) together from the same blood lines it
could lead to mental illness of some sort. God forbid (Leviticus
18:9-18), marriage is monogamy one man and one woman for life.

Chapter 5

Should Marriage be Motivated by Love?

Many people around the globe believe in marriage because of tradition or usually practical association with the norm of society. The question is, should marriage be motivated by love alone? How many of you know love is a very small reason to say, "I Do". Love is an emotion that fades away over time, I say to you, do not marry for love alone. Marriage should be motivated by two individual agreeing they can best serve God by coming together as husband and wife for spiritual sanctifications for the work of the ministry. Love must be a part of it but God is the ultimate choice, you must first love God before you can truly love someone else. We serve a jealous God. As a matter of fact, He said, "Thou shalt have none other gods before me." A "gods" is whatever a people put head of God in their life. Some people literally worship the ground their mate walk upon, they surrender their life goals and dreams to follow their (spouse) dreams. Have you ever read, heard or seen on the news where a spouse killed the other spouse for infidelity. Why or how can that happen? One spouse gives up their entire life goals and dreams to support the other spouse to pursue their career; in most instances they are pursuing a career as a doctor, lawyer or executive officer of a fortune five company. When a spouse does that they should have skills in case a crisis happens and you need to work to make ends meet. Never limited your self where you are unable to work if life dictates that. We never know when God will call one spouse home from labor to rest. With the high rate of divorce in the church you should be prepared for any and all unexpected events to happen. We know optionally God is in control of our lives, but, we also have to deal with an adversary who loves to destroy marriage. Apostle Peter said,

> "Be sober, be vigilant: because your adversary the
> devil, as a roaring lion, walketh about, seeking
> whom he may devour (1Peter 5:8).

Apostle John said, "The thief cometh not, but for to steal, and to kill and to destroy" (John 10:10).

The reality of situation is this, marriage sometime ultimately comes to an end, either by death or by divorce. Each person should bring something valuable into the relationship which can contribute to building a successful marriage and family. You can no long follow old traditional values where the wife stay home and keep house, take care of the kids, and prepare dinner every day. We live in a society where it requires two to live a comfortable life serving God. Therefore, love, looks and financial support is not a true reason to marry. It is paramount both have a careers and equally willing to participate in the marriage financially, mentally and spiritually. Making a vow is a colossal decision, once you spoke the vows God aspects you to honor them unto death.

According the law concerning vows,

> "If a man vow a vow unto the Lord, or swear an
> oath to bind his soul with a bond; he shall not
> break his word, he shall do according to all that
> proceedeth out of his mouth" (Numbers 30:1).

The principle here is not to break your word but to honor your word [vow], nothing is more important than ones own integrity (word). Be caution against hasty decision and hasty vows ones you speak them and commit yourselves to them there is no turning back. Vows are so important to God he said, "Be not rash with thy mouth, and let not thine heart be hasty to utter any thing before God: for God is in heaven, and thou upon earth: therefore let thy words be few" (Ecclesiastes 5:2).

> When thou vowest a vow unto God, defer [delay]
> not to pay it; for he hath no pleasure in fools: pay
> that which thou hast vowed. Suffer [do not let]
> not thy mouth to cause thy flesh to sin; neither say
> thou before the angel [messenger], that it was an
> error: wherefore should God be angry at thy voice
> [excuse], and destroy the work of thine hands"
> (Ecclesiastes 5:4,6)?

The emphasis of this passage is on the folly of empty words been confess before a sovereign God. God expects sincerity and meaningfulness in vows, He is not impressed with foolish of vain vows. The clergy serve as a mediator between God and man in the performing of the marital vows honor him and reverence God as the Almighty.

Love is not what you see on television or outside looking into someone else marriage; it's not embracing, kissing, having pleasure in fondling one another. Love is a <u>feeling</u> that is short term; love is a <u>devotion</u> which is done for a period of time and the person sometime moves on, love is an <u>affection</u> that wears off. Feeling, devotion, and affection describes ones emotions: According to wikipedia-dictionary. com states, "the marriage union is not established on emotions but on commitments, trust, faith and sacrifice for God.

Trust is not something that comes over night it is over the process of time, make sure you tell each other you deepest and darkest hidden secrets about any friends you may share friendship with, some time the devil will bring up pass history to stir up confusion especially if it's negative. Always have faith in your spouse and share every thing with them, it leaves no room for err or concerns. Faith is given by God, "every man is given a measure of faith." The Bible says, "Whoso findeth a wife findeth a good thing, and obtaineth favor of the Lord" (Proverbs 18:22). If you trusted in the Lord for you wife you should have no problems having faith in her, because you have favor with God. "If God be for us, who can be against us?" We walk by faith and not by sight, trusting your wife to always make the righteous decision whether in your present or out of your present in fear of God judgment.

It is a known fact, without the Holy Ghost it is highly impossible for one to successfully deny their flesh for the sake of another. Wit the anointing of God's spirit every thing is impossible, it is important to live a life walking in power of the Holy Ghost, it will lead and guide you into all truth and righteousness.

According to Harold W. Hoehner contributing author of *"The Bible Knowledge Commentary"* states Apostle Paul as saying, "The measure of the husband's love for his wife means seeking the highest good for another person." A husband must be willing to sacrifice his own life for his wife.

The love Apostle Paul is mentioning here is not the <u>Philia love</u>—which means "is general type of love, used for love between family, between friends, a desire or enjoyment of an activity, as well as between lovers."

<u>Agape love</u>—is the love between a husband and a wife, which means—"it is described as the feeling of being content or holding one in the highest regard, to express the unconditional love of God". <u>Agape love</u>—always has the good of the recipient in mind, which is self-sacrificing. I can assure you "It is better to dwell in the corner of the housetop, than with a brawling woman and in a wide house" (Proverbs 25:24).

John MacArthur the author of "**What the Bible says about Parenting**" has this to say about love—love is a submissive spirit. This sort of love is frankly incompatible with the domineering, commanding way many husbands try to assert their rights as head of the family. Apostle Paul uses this description of biblical love, "It is not self-seeking, it is not easily angered, it keeps no record of wrongs. Love does not delight in evil but rejoices with the truth. It always protects, always trusts, always hopes, always perseveres" (1 Corinthians 13:4-7 NIV Study Bible). And, no greater love a man can offer to his wife than by giving his life for her. He can commit to her, have trust in her, and make sacrifices for her; to give his life is the ultimate choice. Remember, love bind two together as one, Adam said in the Book of Genesis, "Bone of my bones, flesh of my flesh she is called woman, become she was taken out of men" (Genesis 2:24). She is your rib; therefore treat her as if it's your body.

> "For no man ever yet hated his own flesh; but nourisheth and cherisheth it, even as the Lord the church" (Ephesians 5:30).

Let me used this old proverb, "Keep God first in your life, love nothing more than God, and all thy ways acknowledge Him, He shall direct your path." For the sake of marriage love is one ingredient need to have a passionate marital relation, but God is the main source for a life lasting marriage. Don't marry for love. The love you give in a marital relationship is not only toward one another but it should always involve God. God is the source of all things without Him life is a risk, it's like walking on a frozen lake covered with a sheet of ice not knowing if it's going to break once you step on it.

After numerous of hours speaking with young people on the subject of marriage it is mind boggling to hear how the institution of marriage is no longer a priority and the scarcities of having a wife in these last days. Even though there's a limited amount of saved men, they (men) feel saved women set their standard so high you sense perfection is the bar, if not, they prefer to stay single longer. Apostle Paul said, "For it is better to marry than burn" [with passion] (1 Corinthians 7:9). It is better not to marry, than to marry and end up looking for a way out of it later in the relationship. "Better is it that thou shouldest not vow, than that thou shouldest vow and not pay (keep it).

Throughout the process of time I had the opportunity to visit many churches in the Apostolic Faith I was totally surprise to notice how many unmarried saved women were with child, and to know there were divorces in the body of Christ. How can this be? The Bible says,

> For this is the will of God, even your sanctification,
> that ye should abstain from fornication [sexual
> immorality]: that every one of you should know
> how to possess his vessel in sanctification and
> honor. For God hath not called us unto uncleanness,
> but unto holiness" (Thessalonians 4:3,4 and 7).

Ask yourselves these two questions: Are you marrying the person to satisfy the needs of your flesh? Or, are you marrying the person because you can best serve God with them as your spouse? It is imperative that both parties are saved by water baptism in the name of our Lord Jesus Christ for remission of sins, be infilled with Holy Ghost with the initiate evidence of speaking in tongue as the spirit of God gives utterance, living a godly life before God, and paying tithes in a local assembly.

Apostle Paul said in 2 Corinthians 6:14-17,

> "Be ye not unequally yoked together with
> unbelievers: for what fellowship hath righteousness
> with unrighteousness? And what communion hath
> light with darkness?"

41

"And what concord hath Christ with Belial? Or
what part hath he that believeth with an infidel?"

"And what agreement hath the temple of God with
idols? For ye are the temple of the living God; as
God hath said, I will dwell in them, and walk in
them; and I will be their God, and they shall be my
people"

"Wherefore come out from among them, and be ye
separate, saith the Lord, and touch not the unclean
thing; and I will receive you."

Personal testimony, before my wife got married I laid down
the principle I believed in, if she could not abide by them we could
not get marry. Principle (1) there is no divorce, (2) no sleeping in
separate room because of angry, (3) no going the bed mad at each
other, work out a solution, (4) never to argue over money, if we
have it fine, if we don't fine too, and (5) keep our business inside
our home. "Be ye angry, and sin not: let not the sun go down upon
your wrath" (Ephesians 5:26).

I suggest everyone have some moral principles they believe in
and make it known before committing to marriage. Many young
marriages are destroyed and divorce happen for those very reasons
mentioned above. I can assure you there is numerous of other
reasons why some marriages do not make it, but eliminate these
reasons and feel comfortable knowing it won't be for them. This
may sound foolish, but the enemy only need a pin hole to come

into to cause hurricane like damages in your lives. "Neither give place to the devil" (Ephesians 5:27).

One final subject we like to discuss before moving onto another chapter "<u>Co-habitation</u>". During the early 70's it was called "<u>shacking</u>" today we want to soften the terminology by using more of a politic term '<u>co-habitation</u>' which is defined—the act of living together and having sexual relationship without being married. Don't be foolish by the wisdom of men saying it's better to live with the person first before marrying them to see if you can live together or not. That is one of the biggest lies ever been told women/men. "Be not deceived." A quote from the 60's, "Why marry the cow when you getting free milk."

Josh McDowell author of "**Why True Love Waits**" writes, two adults living in the same house is not wrong if there is nothing immoral is taking place. Is it sin, no? However, the Bible clearly states, "Abstain from all [every form of] appearance of evil"

(Thessalonians 5:22).

> Amplified Bible (AMP) interpreted it to say,
> "Abstain from evil shrink from it and keep aloof
> [distance] from it in whatever form or whatever
> kind it may be."

Why tempt yourselves? God wants us to flee from immoral behavior and not exposure ourselves to constant temptation, it is not God who tempts man but the devil.

"Wherefore let him that thinketh he standeth take
heed lest he fall. There hath no temptation taken
you but such as is common to man: but God is faith,
who will not suffer you to be tempted above that
ye are able; but will with the temptation also make
a way to escape, that ye may be able to bear it" (1
Corinthians 10:12-13).

As children of God we have to lead by example, we never
know who is watching our lives, or what effect we have on another
person life in the church, by them seeing you co-habitation with
someone it could cause someone else to fall. "Ye are our epistle
written in our hearts, known and read of all men (2 Corinth. 3:2)

Apostle Paul said, "Wherefore, if meat make my
brother to offend [stumble], I will eat no flesh while
the world standeth, lest I make my brother to offend
[stumble] (1 Corinthians 8:13).

Dr. Paul Bobransky the author of *"The Secret Psychology of
How we Fall in Love"* states, many couples fail to stay together
once co-habitation in a relationship, the reason for this is men
make light of the situation because it is instinctually wired in
men not to commit, unless there is overwhelming evidence the
woman will make a great mate for life. Men would rather live a
single life alone with freedom to do as he pleases, if co-habitate
could not definitely have a positive impact on his quality of
life. Dr. Bobransky goes on to say, couple who lives together
prior to marital vows are more likely to divorce at a higher rates

than couple who marry immediately. Eighty five per cent of co-habitation relationship end up in divorce court.

Scriptures to support No co-habitations:

1. Hebrews 13:4 "Marriage is honorable in all and the bed undefiled; but whoremongers and adulterers God will judge"

2. 1 Thessalonians 4:3-4 "For this is the will of God, even you sanctification that, ye should abstain from fornication. That every one of you should know how to possess his vessel in sanctification and honor".

3. 1 Thessalonians 4:7 "For God hath not called us unto uncleanness, but unto holiness."

4. Ephesians 5:3 "But fornication, and all uncleanness, or covetousness, let it not be once named among you, as becometh saints."

5. 1 Corinthian 10:8 "Neither let us commit fornication, as some of them committed and fell in one day three and twenty thousand."

6. Ephesians 5:5 "For this ye know, that no whoremonger, nor unclean person, nor covetous man, who is and idolater, hath any inheritance in the kingdom of Christ and of God."

7. 1 Corinthians 6:18 "Flee fornication every sin that a man doeth is without the body; but he that committeth fornication sinneth against his own body."

8. 1 Corinthians 6:20 "For ye are bought with a price: therefore glorify God in your body, and in your spirit, which are God's.

9. 1 Corinthians 7:2 "Nevertheless, to avoid fornication, let every man have his own wife, and let every woman have her own husband."

10. Matthew 5:28 "But I say unto you, that whosoever looketh on a woman to lust after her hath committed adultery with her already in his heart."

11. Proverbs 5:18-19 "Let thy foundation be blessed: and rejoice with wife of thy youth. Let her be as the loving hind and pleasant roe; let her breasts satisfy thee at all times; and be thou ravished always with her love."

12. Exodus 20:14 "Thou shalt not commit adultery."

13. Matthew 15:19 "For out of the heart preceed evil thoughts, murders, adulteries, fornication, thefts, false witness and blasphemies."

Chapter 6

The Husband
Responsibilities

Every man is not called to be a husband, or to be a father. If, you are called to be a husband God have called you to be the head and the priest of your home. This calling is not an ordinary calling there is a gigantic responsibilities that comes along with been a husband. Apostle Paul said, "Husbands, love your wives, even as Christ also loved the church, and gave himself for it" (Ephesians 5:25). The marital responsibility of husband is to love your wives. The word love in this passage of Scripture represent the highest degree of love which is *agape*—to means the willingness of giving sacrificial on behalf of the husband for the benefit of his wife, without thought of return. The willingness to sacrifice for your wife is symbolic of Christ giving himself for the church on the cross; the husband should be willing to make the same sacrifice for his wife by submitting his life for her. God holds husbands to a higher level of standard for He called us to be the head, we are to lead our wives according to the way Christ loved us, with kindness, meekness, temperance and forgiveness. At no time should there be anybody or anything to hold you hostile from caring for, providing for, protecting or spending time with your wife. She is the best thing that could ever happen to you in your life time other than having a relationship with God. "Dwell with them according to knowledge, giving honor unto the wife, as unto the weaker vessel, and as being heirs together of the grace of life; that your prayers be not hindered" (1 Peter 3:7).

Remember, you ask her to marry you, she took on your last name to share in your life, honor and respect her you do your name. By doing thus, you are consciously saying to her family you will try to provide as well if not better than her father did when she was under his roof. "Therefore shall a man leave his father and his mother, and shall cleave unto his wife: and they shall be one flesh" (Genesis 2:24).

Who should teach men how to be husbands to their wives, and what age should this process start? There are two major roles the Husband hold in the marriage according to Scripture, (1) He is the priest of his home, and (2) He must be an example of a servant leader. These are colossal responsibilities, to be priest it require you to teach your family God's word, how to pray, how to be a servant, and worship and praise God. Always love and be respectful of your wife at all times. The Old Testament serves as an example how the priest took care of the house of God and the people of God. Husbands always keep yourselves undefiled from sin, as Job made sacrifices for his entire family you must do the same, praying asking God for His blessing and favor upon your family. Job chapter 1 and verse 5, "Job rose up early in the morning and offered burnt offerings according to the number of them in his household. For Job said, It may be that my sons have sinned, and cursed God in their hearts." As head of the family your relationship with God have to be above all your household, God honor faithfulness. As husbands leadeth their wife's he must have a good relationship with God keeping himself prayed up, fasting and studying the Word of God faithfully. He must always go to God asking for forgiving of his sins first that his prayers be not hindered, later interceding for his family in prayer. The husband must become the example of Christ; he must be first partaker of every spiritual and natural thing in the family. The husband is the head of the woman he is in a unique position to offer up prayer of protection and covering for his family. Nobody else is in this position can offer that protection, not their father, not their mother and not their pastor. Jesus said, "No man can enter into a strong man's house, and spoil [plunder] his goods, except he will first bind the strong man; and he will spoil [plunder] his house" (Mark 3:27).

Unless the husband is serving sin he renders his power over to the enemy (devil), to do whatever in his house he (devil) so will, even leading the spouse to committing sin. How can the enemy take the husband's anointed power from him? The husband falls out of relationship with God and into sin. "Now we know that God heareth not sinners" (John 9:31) Without confession his prayer will be hinder, this will allow the enemy to captor his house, this will put the whole family at risk. "If we confess our sins, He is faithful and just to forgive us our sins, and to cleanse us from all unrighteousness" (1 John 1:9).

It doesn't matter how strong you are or how well you can fight physically, man nature strength can't protect your family against Satan demonic power.

> "For we wrestle not against flesh and blood, but against principalities, against powers, against the

rulers of the darkness of this world, against spiritual wickedness in high places" (Ephesians 6:12).

It's the husband's responsibility to teach his family God's ways, it's not the wife, she can help but ultimately God charge the husband to lead his family. Yes, the wife can assist with the instruction, only if the husband doesn't take the leading role. More often then none if the father doesn't teach the children Scriptures, how to pray and fast it doesn't carry the same weight if a wife teach. If the husband is not seen reading the Bible most likely the wife won't read either. Apostle Paul made a very profound statement in 1 Corinthians 14:34 and verse 35 saying, "Let your women keep silence in the churches: for it is not permitted unto them to speak; but they are commanded to be under obedience, as also saith the law." What does that mean? During this time period the synagogue was the place of worship and reading of the Scriptures, do to the seating arrangement in the churches (synagogue) men and women sat separately, it would cause a disturbance for a woman to ask her husband a question across the room, therefore Apostle Paul made it clear, a marriage woman should ask her own husband question at home and learn from him. Headship (leadership) is the process of inspiring, motivate and to accomplish a common goal. For example; serving in the military the soldiers common objective in battle is the mission, taking the next hill, defending their site, or destroying something that belongs to the enemy. In business the goal should be satisfying the customers, to have the best products on the market, or just making a large profit. In a family, the goal should be how we can best serve God. The husband responsibilities is (1) he must have a vision for his family (where to live, number of kids, church to attend and vehicles to drive, (2) he must make the hard decisions (Career, lifestyle and major purchases), (3) he must be responsible for his actions (discipline of kids, income and behavior), and (4) he must be out front leading the charge (taking care of home, showing love and being spiritual).

One important statement written out of an article in "*Maranatha Life Marriage Teaching*" (www. maranathalifemarriage.com) states, as a leader the husband is responsible to God for everything that happens in their families, don't try telling God that you delegated it to your wife, He won't listen. The husband is the one God hold responsible and accountable. When Eve ate of the forbidden fruit God did not call Eve, God called to Adam. "And the Lord God called unto Adam, and said unto him where art thou." (Genesis 3:9).

If the husbands fail to teach his family God's ways and they fall into sin, God will go directly to the husband. If the husband reluctantly withhold teaching his wife and children God's ways their blood is on the husband hands. Every thing that happens in the home is the responsibility of the husband. When there is a problem it is up to the husband to seek the Lord for divine guidance to resolve it.

One more interested point brought out from this article, "To lead requires being out in front, it is impossible to lead from behind, all you can do there is push. When you are trying to lead from behind, all you end up doing is following the one you put up front." When you stay up front and lead you set the example, your family may not always listen to what you have to say, but with a certainty they will follow what you do, from seeing it. As for the wife, she has been designed by God to be a follower, and will follow in whatever direction you lead her. This give you the ability to mold and shape her, by passing on the lessons that you have learned from the Word of God.

As a commitment to your new bride it is the husband responsibility to ensure she have a secure home, full of love and a solid foundation to live in. The husband is to love his wife above all other human being, he is to cherish her, treat her with love, and have compassionate affection not only when it convenient for him, but to give her reassurance constantly. Remember, love is not only to be shown in the bedroom when you need your sexual desires fulfilled. You can show it other ways too; i. e. cooking for her, cleaning, washing clothes, running her bath water, and simply listening to her conversation when she need an ear to hear her. She gave up her name for his name, treat her like it's your own body.

Apostle Paul said it like this,

> "So ought man to love their wives as their own
> bodies. He that loveth his wife loveth himself. For
> no man ever yet hated his own flesh; but nourisheth
> and cherisheth it, even as the Lord the church"
> (Ephesians 528-29).

According to John MacArthur book *"What the Bible say about Parenting"*, husbands should never lead their wives into committing any types of sins, nor to create any situation to provoke her to dishonor or disqualify herself from the favor of God through his behavior or condescending conversation.

> "That ye put off concerning the former conversation the old man which is corrupt according to the deceitful lusts. Let no corrupt communication proceed out of your mouth, but that which is good to the use of edifying, that it may minister grace unto the hearers" (Ephesians 4:22 & 29).

> "Let your speech be always with grace, seasoned with salt, that ye may know how ye ought to answer every man" (Colossians 4:6).

Husbands follow these 10 Commandments of Responsibilities:

1. Thou shalt frequently tell thy wife how important and valueable she is to thee (Philippians 2:3).

2. Thou shalt not take thy wife for granted, but will honor and respect her as thy equal (1 Peter 3:7).

3. Thou shalt hold thy wife's love by the same means that thou won it (Song of Solomon 5:10).

4. Thou shat not fail to kiss thy wife every morning (Song of Solomon 8:1).

5. Remember to do all the little things to keep thy wife happy (Matt. 5:37).

6. Keep thin eye on thy own wife, not on thy neighbor's (Proverbs 5:15-20; Job 31:1).

7. Thou shalt make every effort to see things from thy wife's point of view first (Genesis 21:12).

8. Thy highest allegiance, except God, shall be to thy wife, not thy relatives or friends (Genesis 2:24).

9. Thou shalt actively establish family discipline with thy wife's help (Ephesians 6:4).

10. Thou shalt let not no lies or corrupt communication come out of thy mouth to instigate a fight (Ephesians 4:28;31 and Colossians 3:8-9).

Chapter 7

The wives Responsibilities

It is important prior to marrying couples discuss the role each other will play in the marriage relationship; this can eliminate most problems that may arise throughout the union. Can every single detail be discussed absolutely not, at least a foundation can be laid and a plan in place for the things they will considered as being potential stumbling blocks later. It is imperative that some form of dialog take place as a mean of precaution to prevent any major pitfalls. Many times confrontation occurs because there is a lack of communication, religious belief or cultural differences. Don't allow the little foxes to spoil the vine, it is the little foxes that destroys and disrupt marriages, i.e. (1) fighting over money issues, (2) religion, (3) discipline of the kids, and (4) unacceptable behavior (hanging out with old friends, to much debt, working too many hours and spending all your time in front of the television, and not sharing quality time with each other). The wife responsibilities should be of a virtuous woman who exercises great care for her husband and family in the fear of God, according to Proverbs 31 verses 10 through 31. She is rare, her price is far above rubies, and she is priceless. The heart of her husband doth safely trust in her, she is trustworthy. She will do him good and not evil; he is constantly in her love. She worketh willingly with her hands, she is a diligently and hard working. She is like the merchants ships; she is thrifty and conserve. She riseth also while it is night, and giveth food to her household, she is unselfish. She considereth a field and buyeth it, she is an entrepreneur. She girdeth her loins with strength, and strengtheneth her arms, she is not afraid of hard work. She perceiveth that he merchandise is good: her candle goeth not out by night, she willingly to work long hours. She layeth her hands to the spindle, and her hands hold the distaff. She willing to do monotonous work. She stretcheth out her hand to the poor, she is compassionate to those less fortunate. She is not afraid of the snow for her household; for all her household is clothed, she prepare for the future. She maketh herself coverings of tapestry, she is a good seamstress, and she repairs her children clothes. She openeth her mouth with wisdom; and her tongue is the law of kindness, she is wise and kind. Her children arise up, and call her blessed, her husband also, and he praiseth her, so she is blessed by her family. She favor is deceitful, and beauty is vain: but a woman that feareth the Lord, she is a woman of God.

There is rarely a problem in the home when the wives have a strong relationship with Christ, when the wife submit and reverence her husband in all things. The wife is to guide the home on day to day functions; preparing the meals when applicable, keeping the house neat and clean, making sure laundry is complete, nurturing the children (if any), and having a loving spirit filled home. All of these things should take place under normal circumstance if the wife is a stay at home wife, if she work long hours to help support the family all things have to be considered then both parents should share in the day to day functions. At this point she is her husband "help meet" working together for one common goal survival. In such case, the wife responsibilities should change and be equally divide between the spouses, to maintain proper household functions on a daily basic. She is not a slave, she is your wife honor her. As far as their spiritual role goes the husband is still head of the wife, she is not to under exaggerate or compromise the husband position as leader of the family. "For the man is not of woman; but the woman of the man. Neither was the man created for the woman; but the woman for the man. Nevertheless neither is the man without the woman, neither the woman without the man, in the Lord" (1 Corinthians 11:9, 11).

Apostle Paul said,

"I will therefore that the younger women marry, bear children, guide [manage] the house, give none [no opportunity] occasion to the adversary to speak reproachfully" (1 Timothy 5:14).

"To be discreet, chaste, keepers at home, good, obedient to their own husbands, that the word of God be not blasphemed" (Titus 2:5).

Wives keep the honeymoon going never withdraw for showing intimacy toward your husband, the fire should never go out it may go down but never let it go out completely. You were made to satisfy him emotionally, physically and sexually. Solomon said, "Let thy fountain be blessed; and rejoice with the wife of thy youth. Let her be as the loving hind and pleasant roe; let her breasts satisfy thee at all times; and be thou ravished [intoxicated always with her love" (Proverbs 5:18-19).

Ravished—means "intoxicated and exhilarated." This verse shows that the sexual relationship in marriage exists for pleasure as well as procreation.

Apostle Paul said,

> "The wife hath not power of her own body, but
> the husband: and likewise also the husband hath
> not power of his own body, but the wife. Let the
> husband render unto the wife due benevolence
> [affection]: and likewise also the wife unto the
> husband" (1 Corinthians 7:4, 3).

Wives follow these 10 Commandments of Responsibilities:

1. Thou shalt honor thy husband as thy head.

2. Thou shalt communicate with thy husband at all times.

3. Thou shalt not deny thy husband his due benevolence.

4. When there is a problem thou shalt speak with each in love.

5. Thou shalt not covenant thy neighbor husband.

6. Thou shalt not manipulate your husband for sex to get money or vacation.

7. Thou shalt keep no secrets or hide anything of importance from thy husband.

8. Thou shalt always sleep together and not apart at no time.

9. Thou shalt never allow family or friends come in between the relationship under no circumstances.

10. Thou shalt show love and kindness to each other always unto death.

Chapter 8

Divorce, No Divorce

Divorce is thee most controversial conversation today and during Jesus time. This question have caused division and disputing among denominational groups globally. The Pharisees came tempting Jesus with this difficult question "Is it lawful for a man to put away [divorce] his wife for every cause [any reason]? (Matt. 19:3) They were testing the wisdom of Jesus, Jesus proves to be far superior beyond their ex-pectation. Saying, "Have you not read that he which made them at the beginning made them male and female". And said, for this cause shall a man leave father and mother, and shall cleave to his wife: and they twain shall be one flesh? Wherefore they are no more twain, but one flesh. What therefore God hath joined together let not man put asunder [separate]" (Matt. 19:4-6).

The Bible is crystal and infallible God don't make mistake nor contradict his Words. In other words, with God there is no divorce, but with man they permitted it. God said, "I hate divorce" (Malachi 2:16). If you are a believer in Jesus Christ and call yourself a 'Christian' christlike you should not believe in divorce either. According to American Heritage Dictionary-divorce-means "legal dissolution of a marriage"; (2) to dissolve the marriage between man and woman; (3) to end marriage with one spouse; and (4) to cut off or separate.

The Pharisees said to Jesus, "Moses suffered [permitted] to write a bill of divorcement, and to put her away [dismiss her]"

(Mark 10:3). But Jesus answer them saying, "For the hardness of your heart he wrote you this percept [law]. But from the beginning of the creation God made them male and female. Whosoever shall put away [divorce] his wife, and marry another, committeth adultery against her. And if a woman shall put away her husband, and be married to another, she committeth adultery" (Mark 10:4, 11-12). The scriptures in the New Testament book written in Red lettering signify the words of Jesus Christ. Focus should never be on ending a marriage union through the natural laws of man, but searching for the Divine Will of God to continue in the marriage. The question was asked what if you husband or wife committed adultery can they be divorce? Jesus said in Matthew 19:9, "Whosoever shall put away [divorce] his wife, except it be for fornication [sexual immorality], and shall marry another, committeth adultery: and whoso marrieth her which is put away [divorce] doth commit adultery."

The Scripture is saying, whosoever decide to put away their spouse for fornication you can not remarry, be involved in any sexual activities outside of the marriage. Even though man gave you a bill of divorcement under God's divine law you are still married to your husband until he dies. Divorce does not end a marriage only death; divorce only ends the physical living arrangement between the husband and wife. Jesus said, "But if ye do not forgive, neither will your Father which is in heaven forgive your trespasses" (Mark 11:26).

Apostle Paul said,

> The wife is bound by the law as long as her husband
> liveth; but if her husband dead, she is at liberty to
> be married to whom she will; only in the Lord (1
> Corinthians 7:39).

According to Norman Geisler in his book "Christian Ethnics"
states, divorce violates God's design for marriage. God's ideal for
marriage is a monogamous life-time commitment. (Matthew 19:6
and Romans 7:2) Needless to say, divorce breaks a vow made
before God, breaking a sacred vow is wrong. "It is better not to
vow that to vow and not fulfill it" (Ecclesiastes 5:5). The Book of
Malachi second chapter and verse 14 says, "Yet ye say, wherefore"
Because the Lord hath been witness between thee and the wife of
thy youth, against who thou hast dealt treacherously: yet is she thy
companion, and wife of thy covenant."

Jesus condemned all divorces, when Jesus was asked about
divorce in Mark 10:1-9, he gave no exceptions, this was later
affirmed in the Book of Luke 16:18 which states, "Whosoever
[anybody] putteth away his wife, and marrieth another, committeth
adultery; and whosoever marrieth her that is put away from her
husband committeth adultery." Apostle Paul condemns divorce,
he said, "I give command (not I, but the Lord): a woman must
not separate from her husband. But if she does, she must remain
unmarried or else reconciled to her husband (1 Corinthians
7:10-11). Divorce also violates a sacred typology. Why? It destroys
the systematic characteristic of Jesus and the church, the heavenly

marriage between Christ and his bride the church. Symbolically, Christ represent the groom and the church is His bride, Christ has only one bride which is the church and He gave his life for it. Therefore God expects his people (the church) to walk in his statutes and be a light to the world in all things especially in marriage one man one woman for life "until death do ye part". Light of the world describes the essential mission of the people of God's [Christian] to the world, light is to clearly shine forth into the darkness of human depravity. Divorce is one of those moral corruption man have indulge himself in for centuries; God never meant it to be from the beginning.

Spiritual leaders in the church are commission to live an unapproachable life before God and man. First Timothy chapter three and verse 1 and 2 give the qualification of a Bishop. "This is a true saying, if a man desires the office of a bishop, he desireth a good work. A Bishop then must be blameless, the husband of one wife . . ." I believe this to mean only one wife.

After careful reading of John 4 and verse 16 Jesus told the Samaria woman, "Go call thy husband, and come hither. Jesus in his omnipresence power prophesied to the woman says, "For you have had five husbands, and the one whom you now have is not your husband; in that you spoke truly", i.e. one man, one woman for life.

Does God honor unbeliever's marriages? "Marriage is honorable among all" (Hebrews 13:4). No one is exempt believers or unbelievers, Apostle Paul said,

And the woman which hath a husband that believeth
not, and if he be pleased to dwell with her, let
her not leave him. For he unbelieving husband is
sanctified by the wife, and the unbelieving wife is
sanctified by the husband (1 Corinthians 7:13-14).

Therefore, do not be confused or mislead by the myth
unbeliever marriages are not honorable in the sight of God. "God
rain on the just as well as the unjust." For that reason, "let your
conversation be without covetousness; and be content with such
things as ye have (Hebrews 13:5). There is no doubt God has
ordained the sacred relationship of marriage for an approval of
conjugal loyalty between husband and wife.

Divorce destroys the unity of family, it mentally, emotionally
and physically stresses out all parties involves especially children,
it deplete family finances, and it leave deep scares most cases
negatively, i.e. God hate divorces. In Myron Horst book "Divorce
& Remarriage", he discuss what early Christian writers wrote
concerning theologian like Justin Martyr, Clement of Alexandria,
and Tertullian, who philosophy is similarly. Justin Martyr-all
who by human law are twice married are in the eye of our Master
sinners, those who looks upon a woman to lust after her committed
adultery in his heart. Clement of Alexandria-had an "exception
clause" states the only provision for divorce is for a remarried
couple to end their sinful marriage, it legal under the law 'one
man, one woman' for life. Tertullian in his writing said, maintain
the man who put away his wife, and marrieth another, committeth
adultery; and whosoever marrieth her that is put away from her

husband, also committeth adultery. "For he who marries a woman who is unlawfully put away is as much of adultery as the man who marries one who is undivorced. Permanent is the marriage which is not rightly dissolved; to marry, therefore whilst matrimony is undissolved, is to commit adultery."

Richard Patterson Ph. D. from Talbot Theological Seminary who is a well noticeable theology writer in the *"King James Study Bible"* states, the normal coustom of the ancient Near East was for a man to verbally divorce his wife. In contrast, the ancient law of Israel insisted a writing divorcement or a certificate of divorce be given to the wife. This written statement gave legal protection to both husband and wife. Jesus explains elsewhere that Moses' concession was not intended to be taken as license. The only exception given by Christ is for the cause of fornication sexual unfaithfulness. No question, the statement is clear adultery and fornication is a legitimate ground for divorce. However, the legitimacy of the divorce does not necessarily establish the legitimacy to remarriage.

After carefully reading Matthew 19:9 the Scripture never commands one must divorce his or her unfaithful spouse, it only grants them to because of the hardness of their heart (not able to forgive). Dr. Cheryl Lynn Fawcett, the author of "Understand People" states; divorce, not God's desire to end a marriage union "only by death" but in reality we face these challenges in our society today. The prince of this world is an adversary to divine unity of Christianity, there is nothing more destructed to tear a Christian family asunder from the sanctuary of God. Dr.

Fawcett, believes the effects of divorce are like the root system
of a well developed plant. And, there interconnectedness dictates
pain in their being after been pulled apart inevitable and causing
devastating to the entire system. She said, America's divorce
rate of every 1 in 2 marriage is higher than any other developed
nations. We have reach a point in society where marriage is no
longer a universal goal, it have become the ancient history. Dr.
Fawcett goes on to say, while traditional role for marriage have
changed, the Law of God stays the same. "Marriage is for life."

God put in a plan for newly wedded couple to follow to help
them strengthen their marriage as time goes on. In the Book of
Titus chapter 2 and verses 3 and 4 talks about the older women
teaching the younger women how to be wives to their husbands.

> "The aged women likewise, that they be behavior as
> becometh holiness, not false accusers [slanderers],
> not given to much wine, teachers of good things.
> That they may teach [admonish] the young women
> to be sober, to love their husbands, to love their
> children. To be discreet, chaste, keepers at home,
> good, obedient to their own husbands, that the word
> of God be not blasphemed."
>
> That the aged men be sober, grave, temperate, sound
> in faith, in charity, in patient. Young men likewise
> exhort to be soberminded. In all things showing
> thyself a pattern of good works: in doctrine showing
> uncorruptness, gravity, sincerity, sound speech, that

cannot be condemned; that he that is of the contrary
part may be ashamed, having no evil thing to say of
you" (Titus 2:6-8).

For the Lord, the God of Israel, saith that he hateth putting
away [divorce]" (Malachi 2:16). I believe Jesus reaffirmed the
monogamous family and rebuked immorality and divorce during
His ministry. He spoke out for the indissolubility of marriage
between a man and a woman in Matthew 19:4-6.

"And he answered and said unto them, Have ye
not read, that he which made them at the beginning
made them male and female. And said, for this
cause shall a man leave father and mother, and
shall cleave to his wife: and they twain shall be one
flesh? Wherefore they are no more twain, but one
flesh. What therefore God hath joined together let
not man put asunder [separate]."

Even though Moses permitted divorce God never meant it to
be. Jesus said, **"Moses, because of the hardness of your hearts,
permitted you to divorce your wives, but from the beginning
it was not so"** (Matthew 19:8). The beginning of wisdom is the
fear of God. Apostle Peter, the leader of church who Jesus gave
the keys of kingdom made a very profound statement alone with
John to the Pharisees in the Book of Acts 5th. Chapter and verse
29, "We ought to obey God rather than men." Once you divorce
God never permitted either spouse to remarriage, only death ends
a marriage and allows for remarrying. The question everyone is

asking can you divorce? Jesus said, except for fornication. No one ever ask if they could remarry. According to the Scriptures unless your spouse dies you have to live a single life. **"But and if she depart, let her remain unmarried, or be reconciled to her husband: and let not the husband put away [divorce] his wife"** (1 Corinthians 7:11).

Apostle Paul,

> For the woman which hath an husband is bound by the law to her husband so long as he liveth; but if the husband be dead, she is loosed from the law of her husband" (Romans 7:2).

The marriage union is bond which is meant for man and woman to be together for life, if one spouse dies then he/she is free to remarry (only in the Lord).

Chapter 9

Husband & Wife Oneness

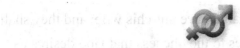

Whether or not you feel one with your wife isn't the issue because oneness isn't based on a feeling. The fact of the matter is this; once you exchange vows God has made you one. At the beginning of creation God saw one thing that wasn't good: "And the Lord God said, it is not good for man to be alone; I will make him a help meet" (Genesis 2:18). God identified an incompleteness of his creation and the answer to this was woman (Eve). Eve was created to multiply humanity and through it make all of creation strong and complete in marriage (this was the plan of God for man and woman), this statement came from the article written by Christopher Barnes on Jan. 19, 2012 "Oneness".

I can see this as a beautiful account of God's first marital union. It was easy for God to have made Adam and Eve at the same time, but He put the man in a position to value the woman after having a good look at the animals. This allowed Adam to see there was no one to whom he could relate with among the creatures. Take a moment to imagine Adam's excitement seeing a mate made for him with such beauty. Even though there will be fundamental physical appearance difference in man and woman, God's design will be such to attract them to each other to enhance their desire for a relationship and bring man and woman together rather than apart. Adam used the term "This is now bone of bones, and flesh of my flesh: she shall be called woman" (Genesis 2:23). This is to indicate the oneness of man and woman together. Let's look at Genesis 2 and verse 24, "Therefore shall a man leave his father and his mother, and shall cleave unto his wife: and they shall be one flesh." This also relates to the oneness that God desires us to have in our marriages.

Three words of interest I like to point out in this above Scripture: (1) what it means to "leave"—it consist of more than distance, it is an attitude of the heart. God's plan for marriage involves oneness. In order for two to become one, they cannot still be attached to anyone else, father, mother, siblings or friends. For them to cleave they must first "leave" their family origin emotionally, physically and mentally), (2) the word "cleave" means to unite with-two bonding together as one. When you think of "bonding" glue comes to mind e.g. super glue-it so strong it makes things stick permanently together. *"The Theological Wordbook of the Old Testament"* gives synonyms for the Hebrew word: **cling to, stick to, stick with, or join to,** and (3) become "one flesh"—this applies to the marriage union sexually. For this to occur you have to leave your parents home and come together by cleaving to each sexually to produce a godly seed in the privacy of your own home. God created sex and procreation to be the fullest expression of that oneness, and the intimacies of marriage are not to be shared with any other human being. A quote of Thomas Adams, "As God by creation made two of one, so again by marriage He made one of two." The prophet Amos said, "Can two walk together, except they be agreed" (Amos 3:3). Here again God is speaking of oneness between the husband and his wife, walking together and agreeing as oneness. There are many caricatures of the Christian point of view regarding the role of husbands head over the wife as master over his slave, wife pregnant barefoot and in the kitchen and taking care of kids. Often time the husband is called the king of his castle causes others to think the rest of the family are silent subjects, scurrying back and forth to carry out the king wishes. Don't be fool by old folk stories, which is as far from the truth as the devil telling the truth. Martha Peace said, "the goal of the Christian husband and wife in their marriage is to have a oneness that is characterized by a loving spiritual and physical bond that glorifies God and thereby enhances personal spiritual growth" (Ephesians 5:22-23). Oneness and spiritual growth are achieved as each partner helps the other become as much like the Lord Jesus Christ as possible. This spiritual growth and oneness in marriage does not happen by chance. It happens in direct proportion to how diligent a couple is in pursuing of God's righteousness. When man and woman comes together in marriage they are closely joined that they become "one flesh", which involves spiritual as well as physical oneness. In marriage God brings a husband and wife together in a unique physical and spiritual bond that reaches to the very depths of their souls. God does this, not man. As God designed it, marriage is to be the welding of two people together into one unit, the blending of two minds, two will, two sets of emotions, and two spirits. "It is a bond the Lord intends to be <u>indissoluble</u> as long as both partners are alive."

What are some of the characteristic husband and wives should institute in their relationship to promote the oneness? To always communicate with one another even when you don't agree on matter or having a verbal confrontation. "Let not the sun do down upon your wrath." When you stop communicating the enemy will speak to one of you and magnified it 10 times greater. (1) Kneel together and pray asking God for direction "all thy way acknowledge Him." (2) Use encouraging words to build up and exhort. (3) Husband, always be quick to apology and be sympathy to her "as unto the weaker vessel" (1 Peter 3:7). Remember, you both are imperfect being subject to mistakes and error, so, let not pride over shadow humility. "A man pride shall bring him low, but honour shall uphold the humble in spirit" (Proverbs 29:23). Never ever try to out shine or embarrass your spouse openly or privately, remember she have your last name. "Put on therefore, as the elect of God, holy and beloved, bowels of mercies, kindness, humbleness of mind, meekness, longsuffering. Forbearing one another, and forgiving one another" (Colossians 3:12). "A house divided can not stand."

-Ways you can stay in the Oneness in God-

1. Don't fight to win an argument pray to keep the devil out of it.

2. Wives/husband be open to compromise (leave open other avenue for later).

3. Agree to disagree (you don't have to win).

4. Submit yourselves one to another (husband take the low road).

5. Schedule time to conversation, pray, and read the Bible together.

6. Plan vacation together.

7. Schedule date nights.

The biblical union of two people into one flesh did not involve the annihilation of personal identity. The unity of marriage is not to be monistic or a unity in duality, but become "one flesh" in oneness. "Two is always better than one".

Chapter 10

Rearing up godly Seeds

The Bible reveals that one key purpose of marriage is the rearing of "godly off-spring" (Malachi 2:15).

> "So God created man in his own image, in the
> image of God created he him; male and female
> created he them. And God blessed them, and God
> said unto them, Be fruitful, and multiply, and
> replenish the earth" (Genesis 1:27-28).

According to the Scriptures man was created by God on the sixth day of creation (Genesis 1:26) and in the grand climax of all that God had accomplished, He joined the material and immaterial parts of man. Man's body was shaped from the dust, but he became a living soul only after God breathed the breath of life into his nostrils (Genesis 2:7). From this the dispensation of innocence the "Edenci Covenant" was established. It was under this covenant, Adam was obligated to replenish the earth with children (Gene. 1:28).

This is why it has been said that "the family is where character is planted and grown. It is the place where civility and respect for others are nurtured and cultivated. God have given parents the commandments and authority to train up their children's to know Him.

In the Book of Deuteronomy which is called the 'book of the second law" God commission father and mother to teach their His laws. Deuteronomy 6:1, 6-9,

> "Now these are commandments, the statutes,
> and the judgments, which the Lord your God
> commanded to teach you, that ye might do them
> in the land whither ye go to possess it. And these
> words, which I command thee this day, shall be in
> thine heart. And thou shalt teach them diligently
> unto thy children, and shalt talk of them when thou
> sittest in thine house, and when thou walkest by
> the way, and when thou liest down, and when thou
> risest up. And thou shalt bind them for a sign upon
> thine hand, and they shall be as frontlets between
> thine eyes. And thou shalt write them upon the post
> of they house, and on thy gates."

God commanded parents to teach their children's his word diligently, it should be a repeated process taught at every opportune time. Teaching is not always by a book, it is by the words you say, how you live your life in front of them, and the way you treat others people. It is imperative parents be in the right relationship with God, members of a local church assembly attends services faithfully, living a God fearing life and studying God's word with much prayer. God holds parents accountable for not teaching their children the righteousness of God at an early age. But Jesus said, Suffer little children, and forbid them not, to come unto me: for of such is the kingdom of heaven" (Matt. 19:14).

David Sorenson author of the book *"Training your Children to turn out Right"* said, "Every Christian parent ought to want their child to grow up to be godly and serve the Lord in the church. This process starts in the home not after the birth but during conception, singing spiritual songs, reading the Bible out loud, and praying openly. Why? It is a scientific fact according to Dr. David B. Chamberlain, Ph.D. in www.birthpsychology.com/lifebefore/fetalsense.html on fetal senses states, a woman fetus can hear at 16 weeks of gestational age. Although the ear is not fully developed until 24 weeks but the structures of the fetal ears begin to form about eight weeks after conception. Dr. Alice H. Cash confirmed research shows that around the beginning of the 4th. month, baby can hear mom's heartbeat, digestive sounds and circulation sounds. Over the next 6 months hearing grows and by the last trimester baby pretty much hears what you hear. At nearly 26 weeks the inner, outer and middle ears are complete and the baby's ears begin taking in the world around him. Therefore, it must be extremely important parents talk and speak positive things into the atmosphere during their pregnancy period. "There is nothing form without a man, that entering into him can defile him; but the things which come out of him, those are they that defile the man" (Mark 7:15). Parents have to be care what you sow into your children gates (ears, eyes and mouth) they shall take root and bring forth unbearable fruits. "For whatsoever a man soweth, that shall he also reap" (Galatians 6:7).

Discipline and punishment is ordained by God it is his way of rebuking and correcting children wicked behaviors. Today our society is divided on whether parents have right to punish (spank, beat, or strike) their kids with a belt, tree switch, or wooden paddle. Should parents spank or not spank their children? This question has raised many eyebrows in our society today. Why? Some believe spanking or any physical form of discipline will produce a negative behavior that could cause mental illness in the child. The Bible doesn't speak about giving your child a few love taps-it is very clear that certain things that a child might do call for harsher punishment.

> "Withhold not correction from the child: for if thou
> beatest him with rod, he shall not die. Thou shall
> beat him with the rod, and shalt deliver his soul
> from hell [sheol]" (Proverbs 23:13-14).

Notice what the Lord is saying, the father is not to 'spare' the rod, but he is to make sure that a real chastening [to his backside] has been administered. Quoting Hudson Taylor out of the book "Training your children to turn out Right", "An undisciplined person will never amount to anything in God's work".

Throughout the Holy Bible God judged and punished people for their sins [wickedness] and transgressing the laws of God. Sin requires judgment, and judgment involved punishment "all disobedient is sin". The word 'beatest'—does not imply a violent assault as is the definition in modern English. It speaks of a methodical application of a switch (off a tree) or belt to the posterior (butt/backside).

Apostle Paul said,

> "Now no chastening [discipline] for the present
> seemeth to be joyous, but Grievous: nevertheless
> afterward it yieldeth the peaceable fruit of
> righteousness unto them which are exercised
> thereby" (Hebrews 12:11).

God believes in discipline, when Jesus the Son of God took on the sins of the world the Bible says,

> "Yet it pleased the Lord to bruise him [Jesus]; he
> hath put him to grief: when thou shalt make his soul
> an offering for sin, he shall see his seed, he shall
> prolong his days, and the pleasure of the Lord shall
> prosper in his hand" (Isaiah 53:10).

> He that spared not his own Son, but delivered him
> up for us all, how shall he not with him also freely
> give us all things? (Romans 8:32)

David Sorenson writes, the Bible reveals God's word routinely assures spanking is proper form of punishment for a rude and undisciplined child. According to the following Scriptures:

1. Proverbs 19:18 "Chasten thy son while there is hope, and let not thy soul spare for his crying."

2. Proverbs 22:15 "Foolishness is bound in the heart of a child; but the rod of correction shall drive it far from him."

3. Proverbs 23:13 "Withhold not correction from the child: for if thou beatest him with the rod, he shall not die."

4. Proverbs 29:15 "The rod and reproof give wisdom: but a child left to himself bringeth his mother to shame."

5. Proverbs 12:6 "For whom the Lord loveth, he chasteneth and scourgeth every son whom he receiveth."

Have you notice parents are no longer rearing their children according to normal family tradition. There is more teenage doing what mothers or fathers should do in the home individually and with siblings more so then parents. What do I mean by this? There are more 8 and 10 year old kids cooking their own breakfast, washing their own clothes, and selecting their own clothes to wear to school. What happen to the days when your mother woke up early to make breakfast, pray with you and hug you before sending their kids off to school? The father's would come home from work and check the kids school work to make sure they understood their assignments every school night. You read more about young kids on drugs, in gangs or being abducted by someone from been on the internet to often.

Parents, you can not allow the world, school, babysitters, after school programs and neighbors rear your children. Too much negative things going on in the world parents must solicit their church for help. Most churches have different programs the world have, e.g. tutoring after school, mentorship programs, teen night, young people groups, and round table sessions. The school system can not train your children up in the Lord. The school system does not even want your child praying in school. God charged the parents to "train up a child in the way he should go, and when he is old he will not depart from it" (Provb. 22:6).

What do I meant the school system can not teach your children God way? E.g. the schools teach classes the earth was created by the "Big Bang Theory", the Bible teaches, "In the beginning God created the heavens and the earth" (Gene. 1:1), the schools teach man evolved from an ape, the Bible teaches "And the Lord God formed man of the dust of the ground, and breathed into his nostrils the breath of life, and man became a living soul" (Gene. 2:7). Schools teach success is having a great education, great job, high income, live in a expensive house, and driving a nice car, the Bible teaches, "But seek ye first the kingdom of God, and his righteousness and all these things shall be added unto you" (Matt. 6:33). Schools teach to invest in real estate (home) and purchase stocks, the Bible teaches "God shall supply all your needs according to His riches and glory" (Philippians 4:19).

One more important note on discipline your children establish who's going to perform the physical punishment (father/mother) on the child, decide how many strokes you going to minister to them, and when and how. Never beat you kids publicly or when you are very angry in both cases it sends out a negative messages to the child and to others. It is a true fact, parents who beat their kids while angry or very up-set tends to over punish which result in child abuses, e.g. broken bones, lacerations, or bruised internal organs. It is necessary to discipline your child, but is unnecessary to abuse them to cause minor or serious injuries. Use wisdom and do it in love. "Fathers, do not exasperate your children; instead, bring them up in the training and instruction of the Lord" (Colossians 3:6). There are many case files of child abuse document with local courts, state and local social service departments in practically every state in United States where a normal disciplinary action got out of control in families. When that occurs God is not pleased, He (God) ordained punishment to correct behavior, not to the extreme to cause bodily injuries to the child. "Let all things be done decently and in order" (1 Corinthians 14:40).

-Separation from the world-

Apostle Paul wrote a very profound statement to Roman saints saying,

> "And be not conformed to this world: but be
> ye transformed by the renewing of your mind"
> (Romans 12:2).

Be not conformed "stop conforming yourselves"; you are to resist being poured into the mold of the present thinking, value systems, and conduct of this world. The world is literally "age", referring to a godless system that act, dress, say and do any thing contrary to the Word of God. We are not to accept the pattern of an age whose god is the Devil. What do I mean by that is this, you see so many young people marking all over their bodies with tattoos, we know this to be tricks of the devil. God's moral law required his people not to "make any cuttings in your flesh, nor print any marks upon you" tattoos. When you indulge in practices it defile the temple in a direct way, since Christian collectively and individually are temple of the Holy Ghost and should be respect in the highest degree.

Apostle Paul, He says,

"Wherefore come out from among them (world),
and be ye separate, saith the Lord, and touch not the
unclean thing; and I will receive you.

In a direct respond to the above scripture David Sorenson author of *"Train your children to turn out Right"* writes, the injunction in this text is clear, we are to sepa-rate ourselves as God's people from the world systems (material things e.g. tattoos etc.) but also ungodly people (sinners) who choose not to follow after God. As people of God we ought not to go into place the world go, e.g. night clubs, bars, strip clubs and gambling halls. Christian (saints) is called to be the 'light of the world' be example to illuminate Jesus for the world to see and follow. "We are peculiar people" (1 Peter 2:9), the world should want what we have.

Sadly to say, the world appears to our young people so strongly they yearn to taste what they are offering, it is the duties of

Christian parents to quench that thirst. There's a theory you can believe in, when two people comes together not of the same spirit (belief) someone is going to pull the other to follow or conform to the things they practice (lifestyle). As a personal testimony I can confirm to the theory, I was a victim of circumstance. One story that comes to mind is Lot the nephew of Abraham (father of faith), the Bible does not indicate whether Lot followed after God once he went into Sodom and Gomorrah, nor does it states Lot knew of the life style of the people there. Sodom and Gomorrah typifies this presence world with all the sinning that is going on now is clearly a reminder of the judgment to come. The point is this, Lot and his family had so much of Sodom and Gomorrah in them when God sent the angels (2) to destroy those cities only 3 members of Lot's family of 10 was saved. My gospel mother (Pastor Marie D. Battle) told me years ago (1977) "wear this world as a loose garment, but get rooted in the Word of God." I ponder that for years, I learned this material world is going to pass away, but God's word is for eternality. It's better to be in Jesus than becoming a part of this world. Jesus said, "For what shall it profit a man, if he shall gain the whole world, and lose his own soul" (Mk 8:36).

The more churches teach separation the more it seen the world creeps into the churches, e.g. rap gospel, dancing, and dress down. The Bible do not speak of rap, it do say, make a joyful noise which involves singing "not rapping". Shouting is spiritual, dancing is worldly. Dress down, come as you are is not Scripture as some would have you to believe, the Bible says, "Whosoever will let him come." (Rev. 22:17). God is calling for our best at all times when we come into his presence, He gave the world his best Jesus Christ

and his Holy Spirit. When the priest came to offer up sacrifices
for the Israelites he had to wear the priestly garments, the animal
sacrifice could not have any blemishes. If the sacrifice animals had
to be perfect man is much more made into God image, God expects
our best. We are to dress in modest appeals re-membering we
ambassadors of God, not to dress too extravagant or ostentatious to
offend others.

Does it make anyone uneasy to see young Christian men
and women dressing in the latest fad of the world, e.g. shoes,
hairstyle colors, short skirts and boys' tight pants? Parents, there
is a message in the clothing, hairstyle, and shoes before you
purchase them research the history behind them first. Some styles
are not for Christian, e.g. the history behind the women high
shoes is to silently let men know they are prostitute, along with
the different colors of hair, the short skirt is very inviting for the
same (prostitution). The tight pants for men are a sign he is gay
(homosexual) or entertained other men.

Apostle Paul said,

> "All things are lawful for me, but all things are not
> expedient: all things are lawful for me, but all things
> edify not" (1 Corinth. 10:23)

Here we see Apostle Paul is speaking in restricted sense, we
can not do the things we see the world do, we are ambassadors of
an Higher Power and our conduct and character should portrait
that. The clothes, shoes and hairstyle is a strong indication where

their heart is or turning toward, parents your obligation is to steer them back toward the things of God. The fewer parents allow the world into there home the greater the chances are for your children to serve God. Conversely, we know separation from the world is highly impossible or practical, but parents are to do every thing in their power to keep your children in church, prayer, reading the Bible and working in the church as much as possible. It is your duty to keep your child before God in prayer every day, and fast for your children God keep them in His will. It is extremely impossible to shield your children from every thing going on in the world, you can monitor the things they bring into your home, the places they go, the friends they keep, what they watch on T.V. and what website they visit on the internet. The more church activities (e.g. Sunday school activities Bible bowl, young people ministry, choir, praise and worship leaders, and music ministry etc.) you involve them God will be more of their focus.

We have to remember kids have problems too never think they are too young to stress over life challenges. Today we hear and see young people committing suicide over stressful and depressing situation in their lives, without parents having knowledge of their stressful and depress state the child is in, this is a serious issue. No one really understands what a child goes through on a day to day basic unless you communicate with them daily. Parents don't ever be too busy to have discussion with your kids to see what's going in their lives (school, friends, social activities, and day to day life), always be quick to hear and give whatever help necessary to resolve it. If you don't make time the devil will for sure send someone who will give them the wrong advice. It's "the little foxes that spoils the vine" (Song of Solomon 2:15). Your child is your gift from God cherishes them and always shows them love. Having a relationship with your children should always be the concern of the parent, make yourself available for them to approach you with any issues or situation going on in their lives. Communication can and do save lives, parents should never cast them aside because of their own agenda. Always leave the door open for them to come through when they feel a need to talk about their troubles. If and when they do come please keep the conversation positive and assure them every thing will work out for their good, if you become negative or combated you will never get the opportunity again for them to trust you. Use wisdom, seek God for direction He will direct your path. Remember, God holds parents responsible for the gift (child) He put them in your charge.

Chapter 11

Intimacy in the Marriage

Did God ordain marriage for sex alone? Apostle Paul said, "I say therefore to the unmarried and widows, it is good for them if they abide [remain] even as I. But if the cannot contain, let them marry: for it is better to marry than to burn" (1 Corinth. 7:8-9). The subject marriage and sex in the Bible is one topic I was not sure to include in this book. However, after some personal experiences and hearing testimony of other married men I thought it was an opportune time to speak on it. The sex drive is an unforeseen force that greatly influence the way we behave as a society. Without the desire of sex neither you nor humanity would exist today. Sex was created by God so we could multiply and replenish the earth (Gene 1:28). God's plan before creation was to make male and female for the sole purpose of procreation. The desire for sex is God ordained for coming together of man and woman into a sexual relationship in the boundary of holy matrimony to consummate the marriage. In this way, the sexual union between husband and wife can bring glory to God as it is experienced in fulfillment of God's design and purpose to provide pleasure, companionship, intimacy, and a means of fulfilling the command of God in producing a godly seed. When God created man every thing he did was to glorify God even in sex fulfilling God purpose for procreation. This fulfilled God's created order having a marital covenant between male and female for life.

"Therefore shall a man leave his father and his
mother, and shall cleave unto his wife: and they
shall be one flesh" (Gene. 2:24).

The one flesh represent a numbers of implications including;
sexual union in marriage, child conception, spiritual and emotional
intimacy. Through these things the secular world should see God's
divine will in oneness at work between husbands and wives in
love.

Jay E. Adams Ph. D. in theology is a well known reformed
Christian author who has written more than 100 Christian books,
said,

Sexual union is not (as some who study the Bible
carelessly think) to be equated with the marriage
union. Marriage is a union that implies sexual union
as a central obligation and pleasure. Both husband
and wife have conjugal rights and exclusive
possession of the other in this area. Nonetheless, a
marriage is consummated when a man and woman
indulges into sexual relations with each other.

God wants each person in the marriage union to
conscientiously fulfill his or her mate's sexual desires. When God
created male and female he planted strong sexual desires to exist
in them for the purpose of coming together sexually for pleasure,
enjoyment and to reproduce of their kind. It is very important
marriage couples understand their partner sexual desires and make

ever attempt possible to satisfy their mate needs. Wives are to set the atmosphere conduce to having sex, e.g. lights dim, bed spread pulled back, dress in her sexiest attire, his favorite perfume, and looking glamour (doll up). Why? Men are sexual aroused by what they see and how one smell. One of the purposes of marriage is to have an outlet for your sexual desires. If one person in a marriage denies his/her partner sex, that may opening the door for temptation. "Neither give place to the devil" (Ephesians 4:27).

Apostle Paul said it like this,

> Let the husband render unto the wife due
> benevolence: and likewise also the wife unto the
> husband. The wife hath not power of her own body,
> but the husband: and likewise also the husband hath
> not power of his own body, but the wife. Defraud
> ye not one the other, except it be with consent for
> a time, that ye may give yourselves to fasting and
> prayer; and come together again, that satan tempt
> you not for your incontinency" (1 Corinth. 7:3-5).

Sex was meant to be a beautiful way for a couple to express their love for each other while nourishing and growing a family of their own. I can say with a reasonable degree of certainty God approved of sex within the confinement of a marriage, and He disapproved of all other forms of sex outside or before marriage. Sex between husband and wife is the ideal order; it is the only sexual means God have officially ordained for humanity for procreation. To enjoy a healthy sexual relationship never do the following things in your bedroom; never argue there, never discipline your kids there, never pay bills there, and never allow the kids to sleep with you there. Sex between husband and wife is supposed to pleasurable, exciting, enjoyable and compassionate. Don't attempt to use sex to manipulate your spouse in doing something they had no intend of doing, that is witch craft (1 Samuel 15:23). Using sex for personal gain is repulsive and eventually will destroy the relationship, the marriage will suffer tremendously and true sexual emotions will become sex for a bargain not in the tenderness of intimacy love. Genuine love is from God always willing to give of yourself looking for nothing in return.

Apostle Paul said,

> Love suffers long and is kind; love does not
> eveny; love does not parade itself, is not puffed
> up; does not behave rudely, does not seek its own,
> is not provoked, thinks no evil; does not rejoice in
> iniquity, but rejoices in the truth (1 Corinth. 13:4-6).

Gary Goodworth wrote this in his article "**Did God ordain Sex**", there is no question that sex influence our world to a great degree, if you don't think so, then why do men do things for attractive woman? Why do women get all dolled up to look pretty when they go out even if they are married? Why do people with money get plastic surgery to keep themselves looking attractive? One answers two words, "sex drive".

God created Adam then made woman from one of Adam's ribs, they had a strong desire for each other and when Adam discovered that Eve had broken the only command that God had given them "not to eat the fruit from the tree of the knowledge of good and evil, Adam had to make a choice. He chose to eat the forbidden fruit because he couldn't bear the thought of losing Eve. Sexual attraction probably had a great influence on his decision. "It is not good for man to be alone" (Gene 2:18). The virtuous wife in the Book of Proverbs chapter 31 and verse 12 says, "She does him good and not evil all the days of her life."

Some people wished they could shed their sex drive so they could truly be free, but remember that it took sex for you and I to be in this world today and it was God who ordained it to be. As long as you stay married keep sex in your relationship, good sex good marriage.

The reality is that we live in a sin scarred world and few couple who marry are virgins (most of today's couple have engaged in pre-marital sex). Ideally, sex should be avoided until both partners marry, you will enjoy it perfectly.

Chapter 12

The Family

When God created humans, he designed us to live in families. In the beginning, God created men and women to live together with one another as husbands and wives, and through their marriage to bring forth a godly seed into the world. As you read in Genesis 3:22-24 it says,

"And the rib, which the Lord God had taken from man, made he a woman, and brought her unto the man. And Adam said, This is now bone of my bones, and flesh of my flesh: she shall be called woman because she was taken out of man. Therefore shall a man leave his father and his mother, and shall cleave unto his wife, and they shall be one flesh."

Family relationship, therefore, are important to God. Even the church, the universal body of believers, is called the family of God. Jesus affirmed the divine institution when he answer one of his disciples concerning his mother and brother at the door. Jesus said,

"Who is my mother? And who are my brethren? And he stretched forth his hand toward his disciples, and said, Behold my mother and my brethren! For whosoever shall do the will of my Father which is in heaven, the same is my brother, and sister, and mother" (Matt. 12:48-50).

God ordained the family as the foundational institution for human society, His standard of living is Holiness. When we receive God's Spirit at salvation, we are adopted into his family. The family is the basic social unit around which everything in society revolves. As the family goes so goes society. If you destroy the family you will destroy civilization. A strong Christian family is the strength of society. It is a blessing to be able to return home to those who love you. The home is where we find spiritual agreement and purpose. Family is where we build Christian character and teach sound doctrine within the privacy of the family unit. Here is where love begins, kindness is shown and loyalty is instilled. Children should be taught to spend their spare time at their own home and not at neighbors' homes. We need to re-member that "be ye ever so humble, there's no place like home."

Good parenting takes sacrifice. It takes a lot of time, it require using wisdom in the mist of a family crisis, having patient waiting on answering from God, and being gentle and kind to one another regardless of the situation. Sacrifice is laying aside your personal agenda for the good of the family. Most importantly, good parenting has unconditional love that can see through the unpleasant behavior and hurtful manipulative words and continue to give your children love in spike of the circum-stance.

When a family is united, it is a good and pleasant thing. Love is the bond that unites us, but we must learn how to restrain our own selfish desire from destroying the family unites. Gary Panell author of the book **"What does God say about Family"**, he said, "family is so important to God he expect husbands and wives to submit themselves one to another in the fear of God." One more important step you need to consider according to Gary Panell, is the sharing of your deepest ideals, kneeling in prayer together night by night, and at the altar rail on Sunday morning encourage-ing each other in everything that is sensitive and fine; offering sympathy and understanding even before it is needed. "A family that is prayerful stays together."

Writer of the article "Christian Family" said, "Unity in Christ is like the dew falling on the mountains, the moisture nourished the vegetation and caused new growth. The plant life supported the animal life and the mountains were lush with God's blessings. When the love of unity dwells in a family, there will also be vibrant life. Children will discover a joy and meaning in life and parents will feel fulfilled in whatever they are doing. And, the dew will fall over the family and nourish spiritual growth. This nurturing environment will cause emotional wholeness spiritually; it will affect our attitudes and help us to be more open to God's divine will for our families." God's love for families is without limits, nothing is held back, He gave his life for the family. "Greater love hath no man than this, that a man lay down his life for his friends" (John 15:13).

One thing I learned prayer is extremely vital for our survival, God desires the best for us and for our families, beside praying for guidance, direction, wisdom, peace and grace, we must constantly pray that our love ones will come into fellowship with the Lord Jesus Christ our Savior. Parents, teach your children to love the Lord in everything they do, every morning before school, in the evening before mealtime, and at bedtime (Deuteronomy 6). Having a family is both an awesome responsibility and a joyous privilege value every moment you have with them (children) you only have them for a short time. The perfect example of a godly family is the virtuous women in Proverbs 31, she not only cares physically for her home, but she is also a "watchman" over the emotional and spiritual condition of her family. Her family member do not feel neglected, they felt blessed.

It is crucial for Christian parents to spend both quality and quantity time with their children. Husbands and wives need to take time out of busy and hectic schedule to have round table discussion with their children, to see if there are problems or needs needed to be address in their lives. Thee most significance decision parents should decide is making every Sunday a day for the entire family go to church to worship and thank God for the many blessing He gave them throughout the week. This should to be an absolute priority. Children need to understand the seriousness of going to church and honoring God the creator. Parents should begin this process by reading with their children at a young age, by reciting parts of the Small Catechism and teaching the Lord's Prayer. The Bible said when Jesus ceased from praying in a certain place one of his disciples said unto Him, "Lord, teach us to pray". And Jesus said unto them,

> "When ye pray, say, Our Father which art in heaven, Hallowed be thy name. Thy kingdom come. Thy will be done, as in heaven, so in earth. Give us day by day our daily bread. And forgive us our sins; for

we also forgive every one that is indebted to us. And
lead us not into tempt-ation; but deliver us from
evil" (Luke 11:2-4).

Parents need to discuss their faith with thief children so they
better understand why or why not they are not allowed to do, to go,
and to wear certain things. Eventually, children will begin to notice
how different they are from other children. Children at school will
tease other kids because of their appearance (dress) and the way
they be-have which is so much different then the other kids. To
protect your children from hurt and disappointment discuss your
religion with them when they are able to comprehend it more. Use
the Word of God as your example when you are explaining things
to your kids, to show them how God expect His people to live
and conduct themselves in life. One more important things family
should do is spend time together every day in the Word of God
(devotional time), learning Scriptures, the 10 Commandments, and
singing Christian hymns together.

A positive attitude toward God provoke a positive outcome
from the Lord, husbands "train up a child in the way he should
go: and when he is old, he will not depart from it" (Proverbs
22:6). God have charged parents to teach their children (family)
about Him through the Word of God (reading, church, and Sunday
school), through their life (prayer, fasting and devotion), and by
their actions (behavior, attitude, and treatment of other people).
Families are the building block God established for the purpose of
continueth of humanity.

Genesis 1 verses 27 and 28 says,

> "So God created man in his own image, in the
> image of God created he him; male and female
> created he them. And God blessed them, and God
> said unto them, Be fruitful, and multiply, and
> replenish the earth, and subdue it . . ."

Conclusion

Marriage, Seeing it God's way. Man did not make marriage; God is the author of it and He ordained it for a man and a woman to enjoy the pleasure of each other in sex.

> "And the rib, which the Lord God had taken from man, made he a woman, and brought her unto the man. And Adam said, This is now bone of my bones, and flesh of my flesh: she shall be called Woman, because she was taken out of Man (unity of one in marriage) Genesis 2:22-23.

The name man and woman is direct correlate with joining together as one in marriage, which is symbolic of a last name (man/woman) she takes on the man name woman as in marriage.

Every man is not a husband and every woman is not meant to be a wife. "But He (Jesus) said unto them, all men cannot receive this saying, save they to who it is given. For there are some eunuchs, which were so born from their mother's womb; and there are some eunuchs, which were made eunuchs of men: and there be eunuchs, which have made themselves eunuchs for the kingdom of heaven's sake. He that is able to receive it let him receive it" (Matt. 19:11-12). This indicates that some are called to be married and remain married; others who cannot accept this are called never to marry.

Apostle Paul said,

> "It is not good for a man not to touch a woman.
> Nevertheless, to avoid fornication, let every <u>man</u>
> have his own wife, and let every <u>woman</u> have her
> own husband" (1 Corinthians 7:1b-2).

Sexual intercourse is more than a physical experience; it involves a communion of life. Since Jesus is one with the believer's spirit, it is unthinkable to involve Him in immorality. Sexuality is a uniquely profound aspect of the personality, involving one's whole being. Sexual immorality has far-reaching effects, with great spiritual significance and social complications.

This is to say, one man for one wife, and one woman for one husband to avoid premarital sex. Sex outside of marriage is not of God but of man's flesh. Flee fornication. Every sin that a man doeth is without the body; but he that committeth fornication sinneth against his own body (1 Corinth. 6:18). Do you not know your body is the temple of the Holy Ghost, which is in you, which ye have of God, and ye are not your own? Jesus paid the price for all sins, therefore glorify God in your body, and in your spirit, which are God's. (1Corinth. 6:19-20)

Such immorality is not only a sin against the body; it is a sin against the Holy Spirit, who dwells in the body.

We covered many subjects in the book on marriage and family according to the Word of God. God has always meant for man and woman to be together for life and rear up godly seed to continue humanity. Society has woven many things into the plan of God to corrupt what He have ordained from the beginning (Genesis 1:26-28; 2:18, 21-24) man and woman together in marriage. Marriage is commitment first to Jesus Christ and then to each other (husband and wife). No where in scriptures God allowed man to marry more than one wife without judgment for their sins? Even when Abraham and Sara fail to trust God for his heir the handmaid Hagar who Sara gave unto her husband was trouble which caused them to put her out of the camp once Ishmael was born. More than one wife stirs up many kinds of problems in the family; therefore God is not in favor of it and disapprove of it. Polygamy is not permitted by God. Remember, the essence of marriage is that two people become one flesh. And one is the indivisible number. In Matthew 19:5 Jesus quoted Genesis 2:24 "Therefore a man shall leave his father and mother and be joined to his wife, and they shall become one flesh." The Hebrew word translated "be joined" refers to an unbreakable bond. It indicates that marriage is meant to be 2 people diligently and utterly committed to pursuing one another in love, bonded in and insoluble union of mind, will, spirit and emotion.

God is so powerful he could have filled the earth with men and women as he did the fishes in the waters and animals Adam named. God wanted man and woman to multiply reproduce their on kind together (Genesis 1:26-28).

Children are a gift from God they are to be taught to reverence Him for the many blessing He continue to give them in life.

Parents are charge to train up a child in the way they should go using Jesus as their example. More so now than ever before, Christian parents need to know what the Bible say about parenting and rearing a godly seed. Many parents today seek answers from all different kinds of secular source calling themselves experts in mental health psychiatry or orthopsychiatry to rear their children, all they need is the Word of God.

Looking to the secular world for answers in rearing your child is as a minefield strewn with danger and emotional hazards. Many problems in the family is not mental illness but demonic in nature. It is recorded on many occasions that Jesus did demonic deliverance; it was not hidden or strange. 1 John 3:8 "For this purpose the Son of God was manifested, that he might destroy the works of the devil."

John MacArthur said this, "What the Bible says about parenting is not a book on child psychology, nor is it proposing a new parenting method. It is simply presenting the principles of biblical parenting with as much clarity as possible."

In the book of 2nd Peter chapter 1 and verse 3 states,

> "According as his divine power hath given unto
> us all things that pertain unto life and godliness,
> through the knowledge of him that hath called us to
> glory and virtue."

I am convinced that if Christians live according to the Word of God their lives will be peaceful, their marriage will endure, and their children will live godly lives. We must submit ourselves to God's ways and He will provide our very needs. I pray this book have opened up your eyes and given you a clearer understanding of Marriage, Seeing it God's way.

God said,

> For my thoughts are not your thoughts, neither are your ways my ways, saith the Lord. For as the heavens are higher than the earth, so are my ways higher than your ways, and my thoughts than your thoughts.

Marriage

Marriage is every woman dream, the longer you live the more it
should become a reality that will change their life.
Marriage is more important than having someone to wake up to,
than having sex with, than saying I love you, than success, than
failure, than what society say it ought to be.
Marriage is more important than self, family, friends and children,
it is an ever lasting union between a husband and wife in oneness.
Marriage is not a covenant that can be easily broken or terminate
by man.
What God joined together let no man put asunder. We cannot
change what
God has established, ordained and sanctified to be.
Man cannot change the inevitable, the only thing we can do is obey
God's percepts and keep his commandments.
I am convinced all marriages are honorable in God and for life.
The remarkable things about God he afford us the opportunity to
marry or stay single, it's a choice we choose. "But, it's better to
marry than burn."
Marriage is 0 percent self, 100 percent giving to your wife, God
designed man to love and cherish his wife, as Christ so loved the
church.
Wives submit to your own husband's and reverence him in all things.
Marriage is a spiritual union between husband and wife serving
God together in the beauty of holiness.
Marriage is for life, there is no divorce. Jesus said, "It was never
meant to be."

The following information was researched by Dr. Brian Wagner B.A. MDiv., ThM., and a PhD. Candidate who is a professor at Virginia Baptist College in Fredericksburg, Va. Bro. Wagner teaches theology and many other seminary courses there. Bro. Wagner contribute the charts and the comparison "It is always wrong to pursue getting a Divorce."

Three definitions as a frame of reference:

(1) <u>Marriage</u>-is the joining of a man and a woman by the threefold action of forsaking parental control, vowing a lifelong commitment, and initiating a one-flesh experience together. The state and the church set standards by which they recognize marriage, but they do not create the marriage bond.

(2) <u>Divorce</u>-is a public sanction that says society will recognize that a couple's marriage, is dissolved by the courts. (The acceptability, as far as society is concerned, of a divorced person marrying again is also assumed.) But divorce is a divine sanction, therefore the courts do not end the marriage bond in God sight the court recognize they no longer can live together as husband and wife, and release them from the agreement.

(3) <u>Sin</u>-is any action of the will of man that does not conform to the will of God. It is one who transgresses God's laws willingly. It is always wrong to pursue any action that goes against percepts of God's Law. His commandments are a

declaration of His will. Bible examples are not commands, and cannot be used as justification to disobey a clear command of Scriptures. Bible example are not commands, nor can they we used to justify ones disobedient to a clear command of Scriptures.

8 Reasons Not to Pursue Divorce:

1. God's original intention was that marriage was to be permanent.

2. God's law demonstrates that bad beginnings in a man and woman's lawful marriage are no excuse for seeking divorce.

3. God's permission of divorce to continue without a prescribed civil penalty is also not excuse to seek that which wrong.

4. Ezra's command to "put away" foreign wives in Ezra's time is no excuse to seek divorce, since it may have not been divorce then, and 1 Corinthians 7 prohibits divorce now.

5. God's "divorce" of Israel is no excuse to seek divorce since God is the only "truly" innocent party, and can justly do things impermissible to man. He also promises reconciliation with Israel.

6. God hates the breaking of the marriage covenant made before Him.

7. Jesus commands not to break the marriage bond since remarriage is an act of adultery.

8. The Holy Spirit (Ghost) repeats through Paul the command of the Lord not to pursue divorce.

(See the chart for Scriptures support on "It is always wrong to Pursue Getting a Divorce" both Old & New Testament books speaks against divorce) Also, after the Charts there are key terms, <u>Argument</u> for and <u>Argument against</u>, "What God had joined together let no man separate" Matt. 19:6.

Bibliography

1. **Brindle, B.A., Th. M., Dallas Theological Seminary, (Many Contributing Editors) *"The New King James Study"*, by Liberty University, copyright 1988.

2. Jay E. Adam, *"Marriage, Divorce, and Remarriage in the Bible"*, by Zondervan Publishing, copyright 1980.

3. Norman Geisler, *"Christian Ethnics"* by Baker Academic (A division of Baker) Publishing Group, copyright 1989.

4. Chad Brand Ph. D., Charles Draper Ph. D., Archie England Ph. D., *"Holman Illustrated Bible Dictionary"* by Holman Bible Publisher copyright 2003.

5. Earl D. Radmacher, Th. D., Ronald B. Allen, Ph. D., H. Wayne House, Th. D., J.D. *"Thomas Nelson Study Bible"*, by Thomas Nelson Publishers copyright 1997.

6. Willard R. Harley Jr., www.gotgustions.org 2010.

7. John F. Walvoord, Roy B. Zuck, *"The Bible Knowledge Commentary"*, by International Bible Society, copyright, 1973, 1978, and 1984.

8. John MacAuthur, *"What the Bible say about Parenting"*, by Word Publishing, Thomas Nelson, Inc. copyright 2000.

9. Josh McDowell, *"Why True Love Waits"*

10. Paul Bobransky Ph. D., *"The Secret Psychology of How we Fall in Love"*

11. John Harley Ph. D., *"Building Marriages to Last a Lifetime"*

12. John C. Maxwell "The 17 Indisputable Laws of Teamwork", by Maxwell Motivation, Inc. Publisher Thomas Nelson, Inc., copyright 2001.

13. Margery S. Berube, Robert B. Costello, Kaethe Ellis, and Marion Severynse, *"American Heritage Dictionary"*, by Houghton Mifflin Company, copyright 1993, 1997.

14. Myron Horst, *"Divorce & Remarriage"*

15. Kenneth L. Barker, John H. Stek, Walter W. Wessel, and Richard Patterson, Ph. D., *"New International Version"* NIV by, International Bible Society, copyright 202.

16. Cheryl L. Fawcett, Ph. D., *"Understanding People"*, by Christian Education at Christian Heritage College, copyright 1995.

17. David Hoehl, Brent Nelson, Jeff Schulte and Lloyd Shadrach, by Gospel Light (A divison of Campus Crusade for Christ), copyright 1997.

18. Website www.townhall.com\col03ists\dennisprayer\2006\10103 \five-non-religious

19. Website www.maranathalife.com

20. Website www.birthpsychology.com\lifebefore\fetalsense.html, by Douglas S. Winnail *"Marriage & Family"*

21. Website www.marriagemission.com\christian.marrying-young-should-we National Healthy Marriage Resource Center

22. Website www.wagnerleadership

Scriptures to Follow

Family:

Genesis 2:18-25
Exodus 20:12
Joshua 24:15
Psalm 103:17
Psalm 127:3-5
Proverbs 128:3
Proverbs 1:8
Proverbs 11:29
Proverbs 12:7
Proverbs 15:20, 27
Proverbs 22:6
Matthew 19:29
Mark 3:23-25
1 Timothy 5:8

Woman & Husband:

Deuteronomy 17:17
Esther 1:20-22
Malachi 2:14-15
Matthew 19:4-12
Mark 10:7-8
Acts 18:8
Romans 7:2

Romans 8:15
Romans 9:4
1 Corinthians 7:10-12; 16
1 Corinthians 7:27-28
1 Corinthians 7:36-39
Ephesians 1:5
Ephesians 2:19
Ephesians 3:14-15
Ephesians 6:1-2
Colossians 3:20
1Timothy 3:2-5
Titus 1:6
Hebrews 13:4
1Peter 5:13-14